PROBLEMS OF THE THEATRE

AN ESSAY AND

THE MARRIAGE OF MR MISSISSIPPI

A PLAY BY

Friedrich Dürrenmatt

GROVE PRESS, INC. NEW YORK

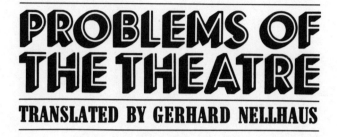

PROBLEMS OF
THE THEATRE

TRANSLATED BY GERHARD NELLHAUS

PREFACE: PROBLEMS OF THE THEATRE

BEHOLD the drive for purity in art as art is practised these days. Behold this writer striving for the purely poetic, another for the purely lyrical, the purely epic, the purely dramatic. The painter ardently seeks to create the pure painting, the musician pure music, and someone even told me, pure radio represents the synthesis between Dionysus and Logos. Even more remarkable for our time, not otherwise renowned for its purity, is that each and everyone believes he has found his unique and the only true purity. Each vestal of the arts has, if you think of it, her own kind of chastity. Likewise, too numerous to count, are all the theories of the theatre, of what is pure theatre, pure tragedy, pure comedy. There are so many modern theories of the drama, what with each playwright keeping three or four at hand, that for this reason, if no other, I am a bit embarrassed to come along now with my theories of the problems of the theatre.

Furthermore, I would ask you not to look upon me as the spokesman of some specific movement in the theatre or of a certain dramatic technique, nor to believe that I knock at your door as the travelling salesman of one of the philosophies current on our stages today, whether as existentialist, nihilist, expressionist or satirist, or any other label put on the compote dished up by literary criticism. For me, the stage is not a battlefield for theories, philosophies and manifestoes, but rather an instrument whose possibilities I seek to know by playing with it. Of course, in my plays there are people and they hold to some belief or philosophy – a lot of blockheads would make for a dull piece – but my plays are not for what people have to say: what is said is there because my plays deal with people, and thinking and believing and philo-

7

sophizing are all, to some extent at least, a part of human nature. The problems I face as playwright are practical, working problems, problems I face not before, but during the writing. To be quite accurate about it, these problems usually come up after the writing is done, arising out of a certain curiosity to know how I did it. So what I would like to talk about now are these problems, even though I risk disappointing the general longing for something profound and creating the impression that an amateur is talking. I haven't the faintest notion of how else I should go about it, of how not to talk about art like an amateur. Consequently I speak only to those who fall asleep listening to Heidegger.

What I am concerned with are empirical rules, the possibilities of the theatre. But since we live in an age when literary scholarship and criticism flourish, I cannot quite resist the temptation of casting a few side glances at some of the theories of the art and practice of the theatre. The artist indeed has no need of scholarship. Scholarship derives laws from what exists already; otherwise it would not be scholarship. But the laws thus established have no value for the artist, even when they are true. The artist cannot accept a law he has not discovered for himself. If he cannot find such a law, scholarship cannot help him with one it has established; and when the artist does find one, then it does not matter that the same law was also discovered by scholarship. But scholarship, thus denied, stands behind the artist like a threatening ogre, ready to leap forth whenever the artist wants to talk about art. And so it is here. To talk about problems of the theatre is to enter into competition with literary scholarship. I undertake this with some misgivings. Literary scholarship looks on the theatre as an object; for the dramatist it is never something purely objective, something separate from him. He participates in it. It is true that the playwright's activity makes drama into something objective (that is exactly his job), but he destroys the object he has created again and again, forgets it, rejects it, scorns it, overestimates it, all in order to make room for something new. Scholarship sees

8

only the result; the process, which led to this result, is what the playwright cannot forget. What he says has to be taken with a grain of salt. What he thinks about his art changes as he creates his art; his thoughts are always subject to his mood and the moment. What alone really counts for him is what he is doing at a given moment; for its sake he can betray what he did just a little while ago. Perhaps a writer should not talk about his art, but once he starts, then it is not altogether a waste of time to listen to him. Literary scholars who have not the faintest notion of the difficulties of writing and of the hidden rocks that force the stream of art into oft unsuspected channels run the danger of merely asserting and stupidly proclaiming laws that do not exist.

Doubtless the unities of time, place and action which Aristotle – so it was supposed for a long time – derived from Greek tragedy constitute the ideal of drama. From a logical and hence also aesthetic point of view, this thesis is incontestable, so incontestable indeed, that the question arises if it does not set up the framework once and for all within which each dramatist must work. Aristotle's three unities demand the greatest precision, the greatest economy and the greatest simplicity in the handling of the dramatic material. The unities of time, place and action ought to be a basic dictate put to the dramatist by literary scholarship, and the only reason scholarship does not hold the artist to them is that Aristotle's unities have not been obeyed by anyone for ages. Nor can they be obeyed, for reasons which best illustrate the relationship of the art of writing plays to the theories about that art.

The unities of time, place and action in essence presuppose Greek tragedy. Aristotle's unities do not make Greek tragedy possible; rather, Greek tragedy allows his unities. No matter how abstract an aesthetic law may appear to be, the work of art from which it was derived is contained in that law. If I want to set about writing a dramatic action which is to unfold and run its course in the same place within two hours, for instance, then this action must have a history behind it, and that history will be the more extensive the fewer the number of stage characters there

9

are at my disposal. This is simply an experience of how the theatre works, an empirical rule. For me a history is the story which took place before the stage action commenced, a story which alone makes the action on the stage possible. Thus the history behind Hamlet is, of course, the murder of his father; the drama lies in the discovery of that murder. As a rule, too, the stage action is much shorter in time than the event depicted; it often starts out right in the middle of the event, or indeed towards the end of it. Before Sophocles' tragedy could begin, Oedipus had to have killed his father and married his mother, activities that take a little time. The stage action must compress an event to the same degree in which it fulfils the demands of Aristotle's unities. And the closer a playwright adheres to the three unities, the more important is the background history of the action.

It is, of course, possible to invent a history and hence a dramatic action that would seem particularly favourable for keeping to Aristotle's unities. But this brings into force the rule that the more invented a story is and the more unknown it is to the audience, the more careful must its exposition, the unfolding of the background be. Greek tragedy was possible only because it did not have to invent its historical background because, it already possessed one. The spectators knew the myths with which each drama dealt; and because these myths were public, ready coin, part of religion, they made the feats of the Greek tragedians possible, feats never to be attained again; they made possible their abbreviations, their straightforwardness, their stichomythy and choruses, and hence also Aristotle's unities. The audience knew what the play was all about; its curiosity was not focused on the story so much as on its treatment. Aristotle's unities presupposed the general appreciation of the subject matter – a genial exception in more recent times is Kleist's *The Broken Jug* – presupposed a religious theatre based on myths. Therefore as soon as the theatre lost its religious, its mythical significance, the unities had to be reinterpreted or discarded. An audience facing an unknown story will pay more attention to the story than to its treatment, and by necessity then such a play has to be richer in detail and circumstances than one with a known action. The feats of one playwright cannot be the feats of another. Each art exploits the chances offered by its time, and it is hard to imagine a time without chances. Like every other form of art, drama creates its world; but not every world can be created in the same fashion. This is the natural limitation of every aesthetic rule, no matter how self-evident such a rule may be. This does not mean that Aristotle's unities are obsolete; what was once a rule has become an exception, a case that may occur again at any time. The one-act play obeys the unities still, even though under a different condition. Instead of the history, the situation now dominates the plot, and thus unity is once again achieved.

But what is true for Aristotle's theory of drama, namely its dependency upon a certain world and hence its validity relative to that world, is also true of every other theory of drama. Brecht is consistent only when he incorporates into his dramaturgy that *Weltanschauung*, the communist philosophy, to which he – so he seems to think – is committed; but in doing so he often cuts off his own nose. Sometimes his plays say the very opposite of what they claim they say, but this lack of agreement cannot always be blamed on the capitalistic audience. Often it is simply a case where Brecht, the poet, gets the better of Brecht, the dramatic theorist, a situation that is wholly legitimate and ominous only were it not to happen again.

Let us speak plainly. My introducing the audience as a factor in the making of a play may have seemed strange to many. But just as it is impossible to have theatre without spectators, so it is senseless to consider and treat a play as if it were a kind of ode, divided into parts and delivered in a vacuum. A piece written for the theatre becomes living theatre when it is played, when it can be seen, heard, felt, and thus experienced immediately. This immediacy is one of the most essential aspects of the theatre, a fact so often overlooked in those sacred halls where a play by Hofmannsthal counts for more than one by Nestroy, and a Richard Strauss opera more than one by Offenbach. A play is an event, is something that happens. In the theatre everything must be transformed into something immediate, something visible and sensible; the corollary to this thought, however, is that not everything can be translated into something immediate and corporeal. Kafka, for example, really does not belong on the stage. The bread offered there gives no nourishment; it lies undigested in the iron stomachs of the theatre-going public and the regular subscribers. As luck would have it, many think of the heaviness they feel not as a stomach ache, but as the heaviness of soul which Kafka's true works emanate, so that by error all is put right.

The immediacy sought by every play, the spectacle into which it would be transformed, presupposes an audience, a theatre, a stage. Hence we would also do well to examine the theatres for which we have to write today. We all know these money-losing enterprises. They can, like so many other institutions today, be justified only on an idealistic basis: in reality, not at all. The architecture of our theatres, their seating arrangements and their stages, came down from the court theatre or, to be more precise, never got beyond it. For this reason alone, our so-called contemporary theatre is not really contemporary. In contrast to the primitive Shakespearean stage, in contrast to this 'scaffold', the court theatre made every effort to satisfy a craving for naturalness, even though this resulted in much greater unnaturalness. No longer was the audience satisfied to imagine the royal chamber behind the 'green curtain'; every attempt was made to show the chamber. Characteristic of such theatre is its tendency to separate audience and stage, by means both of the curtain and of having the spectators sit in the dark facing a well-lit stage. This latter innovation was perhaps the most treacherous of all, for it alone made possible the solemn atmosphere in which our theatres suffocate. The stage became a peep-show. Better lighting was constantly invented, then a revolving stage, and it is said they have even invented a revolving house! The courts went, but the court theatre stayed on. Now to be sure, our time has discovered its own form of theatre, the cinema. But no matter how much we may emphasize the differences, and how important it may be to emphasize them, still it must be pointed out that the cinema grew out of the theatre, and that it can at last achieve what the court theatre with all its machinery, revolving stages and other effects only dreamed of doing: simulate reality.

The cinema, then, is nothing more nor less than the democratic form of the court theatre. It intensifies our sense of intimacy immeasurably, so much so that the films easily risk becoming the genuinely pornographic art. For the spectator is forced into being a 'voyeur', and film stars enjoy their immense popularity because those who see them come also to feel that they have slept with them; that is how well film stars are photographed. A close up is an indecency.

Just what, then, is our present-day theatre? If the cinema is the modern form of the old court theatre, what is the theatre? There is no use in pretending that the theatre today is anything much more than a museum in which the art treasures of former golden ages of the drama are put on exhibition. There is no way of changing that. It is only too natural at a time like ours – a time which, always looking towards the past, seems to possess everything but a living present. In Goethe's time the ancients were rarely performed, Schiller occasionally, but mostly Kotzebue and whoever else they were. It is worthwhile to point out that the cinema pre-empts the theatre of its Kotzebues and Birch-Pfeiffers, and it is hard to imagine what sort of plays would have to be put on today, if there were no films and if all the script-writers wrote for the legitimate stage.

If the contemporary theatre is to a large extent a museum, then this has definite effects on the actors whom it employs. They have become civil servants, usually even entitled to their pensions, permitted to act in the theatre when not kept busy making films.

13

The members of this once despised estate have settled down now as solid citizens – a human gain, an artistic loss. And today actors fit into the order of professional rank somewhere between the physicians and small industrialists, surpassed within the realm of art only by the winners of the Nobel prize, by pianists and conductors. Some actors are visiting professors of sorts, or independent scholars, who take their turn appearing in the museums or arranging exhibitions. The management, of course, takes this into account when it arranges its playbill more or less with an eye to its guest stars; says the management: what play should we put on when this or that authority in this or that field is available to us at such and such a date? Moreover, actors are forced to move about in many different acting styles, now in a baroque style, now in a classical one, today acting naturalism, tomorrow Claudel. An actor in Molière's day did not have to do that. The director, too, is more important, more dominant than ever, like the conductor of an orchestra. Historical works demand, and ought to demand, proper interpretation; but directors as yet dare not be as true to the works they put on as some conductors are, quite naturally, to theirs. The classics often are not interpreted but executed, and the curtain falls upon a mutilated corpse. But then, where is the danger in it all? There is always the saving convention by which all classical things are accepted as perfection, as a kind of gold standard in our cultural life, with all things looked upon as gold that shine in de luxe editions of the classics. The theatre-going public goes to see the classics, whether they be performed well or not; applause is assured, indeed is the duty of the educated man. And thus the public has legitimately been relieved of the task of thinking and of passing judgments other than those learned by rote in school.

Yet there is a good side to the many styles the present-day theatre must master, although it may at first glance appear bad. Every great age of the theatre was possible because of the discovery of a unique form of theatre, of a particular style, which determined the way plays were written. This is easily demonstrable in the English or Spanish theatre, or the Vienna National Theatre, the most remarkable phenomenon in the German-speaking theatre. This alone can explain the astounding number of plays written by Lope de Vega. Stylistically a play was no problem for him. But to the degree that a uniform style of theatre does not exist today, indeed can no longer exist, to that extent is writing for the theatre now a problem and thus more difficult. Therefore our contemporary theatre is two things: on one hand it is a museum, on the other an experimental field, each play confronting the author with new challenges, new questions of style. Yes, style today is no longer a common property, but highly private, even particularized from case to case. We have no style, only styles, which puts the situation in art today in a nutshell. For contemporary art is a series of experiments, nothing more nor less, just like all of our modern world.

If there are only styles, then, too, we have only theories of the art and practice of the theatre, and no longer one dramaturgy. We now have Brecht's and Eliot's, Claudel's and that of Frisch or of Hochwälder: always a new theory of drama for each dramatic offering. Nevertheless one can conceive of a single theory of drama, a theory that would cover all particular instances, much in the same way that we have worked out a geometry which embraces all dimensions. Aristotle's theory of drama would be only one of many possible theories in this dramaturgy. It would have to be a new *poetics*, which would examine the possibilities not of a certain stage, but of the stage, a dramaturgy of the experiment itself.

What, finally, might we say about the audience without which, as we have said before, no theatre is possible? The audience has become anonymous, just 'the paying public', a matter far worse than is at first apparent. The modern author no longer knows his public, unless he writes for some village stage or some festival of drama, neither of which is much fun. A playwright has to imagine his audience; but in truth the audience is he himself – and this is a danger which can neither be altered now nor circumvented. All the dubious, well-worn, politically misused notions which attach themselves to the concepts of 'a people' and 'society', to say nothing of 'a community', have perforce also crept into the theatre. What points is an author to make? How is he to find his subjects, what solutions should he reach? All these are questions for which we may perhaps find an answer once we have gained a clearer notion as to what possibilities still exist in the theatre today.

In undertaking to write a play I must first make clear to myself just where it is to take place. At first glance that does not seem much of a problem. A play takes place in London or Berlin, in the mountains, a hospital or on a battlefield, wherever the action demands. But it does not work out quite that way. A play, after all, takes place upon a stage which in turn must represent London, the mountains or a battlefield. This distinction need not, but can be made. It depends entirely on how much the author takes the stage into account, how strongly he wants to create the illusion without which no theatre can exist, and whether he wants it smeared on thickly with gobs of paint heaped upon the canvas, or transparent, diaphanous and fragile. A playwright can be deadly serious about the place: Madrid, the Rütli, the Russian steppe, or he can think of it as just a stage, the world, his world.

How the stage is to represent a given place is, of course, the task of the scene designer. Since designing scenes is a form of painting, the developments which have taken place in painting in our time have not failed to touch the theatre. But the theatre can really neither abstract man nor language, which is in itself both abstract and concrete, and scenery, no matter how abstract it would pretend to be, must still represent something concrete to make sense, and for both of these reasons, abstraction in scenic design has essentially failed. Nevertheless the 'green curtain' behind which the spectators have to imagine the place, the royal chamber, was reinstituted. The fact was recalled that the dramatic place and the stage were not one and the same, no matter how elaborate, how verisimilar the stage setting might be. The fact is the place has to be created by the play. One word: we are in Venice; another, in the Tower of London. The imagination of the audience needs but little support. Scenery is to suggest, point out, intensify, but not describe the place. Once more it has become transparent, immaterialized. And similarly the place of the drama to be shown on the stage can be made immaterial.

Two fairly recent plays which most clearly illustrate the possibility referred to as immaterializing the scenery and the dramatic place are Wilder's *Our Town* and *The Skin of Our Teeth*. The immaterializing of the stage in *Our Town* consists of this: the stage is nearly empty; only a few objects needed for rehearsals stand about – some chairs, tables, ladders and so on; and out of these everyday objects the place is created, the dramatic place, the town, all out of the word, the play, the wakened imagination of the spectators. In his other play Wilder, that great fanatic of the theatre, immaterializes the dramatic place: where the Antrobus family really lives, in what age and what stage of civilization, is never wholly clear; now it is the ice age, now a world war. This sort of experiment may be met quite often in modern drama; thus it is indefinite where in Frisch's play, *Graf Öderland*, the strange Count Wasteland abides; no man knows where to wait for Godot, and in *The Marriage of Mr Mississippi* (*Die Ehe des Herrn Mississippi*) I expressed the indefiniteness of the locale (in order to give the play its spirit of wit, of comedy) by having the right window of a room look out upon a northern landscape with a Gothic cathedral and an apple tree, while the left window of the same room opens on a southern scene with an ancient ruin, a touch of the Mediterranean and a cypress. The really decisive point in all this is that, to quote Max Frisch, the playwright is making poetry with the stage, a possibility which has always entertained and occupied me and which is one of the reasons, if not the main one, why I write plays. But then – and I am thinking of the comedies of Aristophanes and the comic plays of Nestroy –

in every age poetry has been written not only *for*, but *with* the stage.

Let us turn from these incidental problems to more basic ones. What do the particular problems look like, which I – to cite an author whom I know at least partially, though not fully – have faced? In *The Blind Man* (*Der Blinde*) I wanted to juxtapose the word against the dramatic place, to turn the word against the scene. The blind duke believes he is living in his well-preserved castle whereas he is living in a ruin; he thinks he is humbling himself before Wallenstein, but sinks to his knees before a negro. The dramatic place is one and the same, but by means of the pretence carried on before the blind man, it plays a dual role: the place seen by the audience and the place in which the blind man fancies himself to be. So also, when in my comedy, *An Angel comes to Babylon* (*Ein Engel kommt nach Babylon*), I picked for my dramatic locale the city in which the Tower was built, I had essentially to solve two problems. In the first place the stage had to express the fact that there were two places of action in my comedy, heaven and the city of Babylon; heaven, which was the secret point of origin of the action, and Babylon the locale, where that action ran its course.

Well, I suppose heaven could have been simply represented by a dark background to suggest its infinity, but since I wanted to convey in my comedy the idea that heaven was not something infinite, but something incomprehensible and altogether different, I asked for the stage background, the heaven above the city of Babylon, to be occupied entirely by the Great Nebula in Andromeda, just as we might see it through the telescope on Mount Palomar. What I hoped to achieve thereby was that heaven, the incomprehensible and inscrutable, would take on form, gain, as it were, its own stage presence. In this wise also heaven's rapprochement with the earth was to be brought out, reiterating the coming together of the two that is expressed in the action through the angel's visiting Babylon. Thus, too, a world was constructed

18

in which the result of the action, namely the building of the Tower of Babylon, became possible.

In the second place I had to think of how to make the stage represent Babylon, the place in which the action unfolds. I found the idea of Babylon challenging because of its timeliness, its Cyclopean big-city character, its New York look with skyscrapers and slums, and by having the first two acts take place along the banks of the Euphrates I wished to hint at Paris. Babylon, in brief, stands for the metropolis. It is a Babylon of the imagination, having a few typically Babylonian features, but in a modernized parodied version, with its modernities – for instance the convenience of electric street-lights. Of course the execution of the scenery, the building of the stage itself, is a job for the scene designer, but the playwright must always decide himself just what kind of stage he wants.

I love a colourful stage setting, a colourful theatre, like the stage of Theo Otto, to mention an admirable example. I have little use for a theatre that uses black curtains as was the fashion once upon a time, or for the tendency to glory in threadbare poverty which some stage designers seem to aim for. To be sure the word is important above all else in the theatre; but note: above all else. For after the word there are many other things, which also rightfully belong to the theatre, even a certain wantonness. Thus when someone asked me quite thoughtfully with respect to my play *Mississippi*, where one of the characters enters through a grandfather clock, whether or not I thought a four-dimensional theatre possible, I could only remark that I had not thought of Einstein when I did it. It is just that in my daily life it would give me great pleasure if I could join a gathering and astonish those present by coming into the room through a grandfather clock or by floating in through a window. No one should deny us playwrights the opportunity to satisfy such desires now and then at least on the stage, where such whims can be fulfilled. The old argument as to which came first, the chicken or the egg, can be transformed in art into the question of whether the egg or the chicken, the world as potential or as rich harvest, is to be presented. Artists might very well be divided then into those favouring the egg and those favouring the chicken. The argument is a lively one. Alfred Polgar once said to me, it was odd that while in contemporary Anglo-Saxon drama everything came out in the dialogue, there was always much too much happening on the stage in my plays and that he, Polgar, would sometimes like to see a simple Dürrenmatt play. Behind this truth, however, lies my refusal to say that the egg came before the chicken, and my personal prejudice of preferring the chicken to the egg. It happens to be my passion, not always a happy one perhaps, to want to put on the stage the richness, the manifold diversity of the world. As a result my theatre is open to many interpretations and appears to confuse some. Misunderstandings creep in, as when someone looks around desperately in the chicken coop of my plays, hoping to find the egg of Columbus which I stubbornly refuse to lay.

But a play is bound not only to a place, but also to a time. Just as the stage represents a place, so it also represents a time, the time *during* which the action takes place as well as the time *in* which it occurs. If Aristotle had really demanded the unity of time, place and action, he would have limited the duration of a tragedy to the time it took for the action to be carried out (a feat which the Greek tragedians nearly achieved), for which reasons, of course, everything would have to be concentrated upon that action. Time would pass 'naturally', everything coming one after the other without breaks. But this does not always have to be the case. In general the actions on the stage follow one another but, to cite an example, in Nestroy's magical farce, *Death on the Wedding Day* (*Der Tod am Hochzeitstag*), there are two acts taking place simultaneously and the illusion of simultaneity is skilfully achieved by having the action of the second act form the background noise for the first, and the action of the first act the background noise for the second. Other examples of how time is used as a theatrical device could be easily recalled. Time can be shortened, stretched, intensified, arrested, repeated; the dramatist can, like Joshua, call to his heaven's orbits, 'Theatre-Sun, stand thou still upon Gibeon! And thou, Theatre-Moon, in the valley of Ajalon!'

It may be noted further that the unities ascribed to Aristotle were not wholly kept in Greek tragedy either. The action is interrupted by the choruses, and by this means time is spaced. When the chorus interrupts the action, it achieves as regards time – to elucidate the obvious like an amateur – the very same thing the curtain does today. The curtain cuts up and spreads out the time of an action. I have nothing against such an honourable device. The good thing about a curtain is that it so clearly defines an act, that it clears the table, so to speak. Moreover, it is psychologically often extremely necessary to give the exhausted and frightened audience a rest. But a new way of binding language and time has evolved in our day.

If I cite Wilder's *Our Town* once again, I do so because I assume that this fine play is widely known. You may recall that in it different characters turn towards the audience and talk of the worries and needs of their small town. In this way Wilder is able to dispense with the curtain. The curtain has been replaced by the direct address to the audience. The epic element of description has been added to the drama. For this reason, of course, this form of theatre has been called the epic theatre.

Yet when looked at quite closely, Shakespeare's plays or Goethe's *Götz von Berlichingen* are in a certain sense also epic theatre. Only in a different, less obvious manner. Since Shakespeare's histories often extend over a considerable period of time, this time-span is divided into different actions, different episodes, each of which is treated dramatically. *Henry IV*, Part I, consists of nineteen such episodes, while by the end of the fourth act of *Götz* there are already no less than forty-one tableaux. I stopped counting after that. If one looks at the way the overall action has been built up, then, with respect to time, it is quite close to the epic, like a film that is run too slowly, so that the individual shots can be seen. The condensation of everything into a certain time has been given up in favour of an episodic form of drama.

Thus when an author in some of our modern plays turns towards the audience, he attempts to give the play a greater continuity than is otherwise possible in an episodic form. The void between the acts is to be filled; the time-gap is to be bridged, not by a pause, but by words, by a description of what has gone on in the meanwhile, or by having some new character introduce himself. In other words, the expositions are handled in an epic manner, not the actions to which these expositions lead. This represents an advance of the word in the theatre, the attempt of the word to reconquer territory lost a long time ago. Let us emphasize that it is but an attempt; for all too often the direct address to the audience is used to explain the play, an undertaking that makes no sense whatever. If the audience is moved by the play, it will not need prodding by explanations; if the audience is not moved, all the prodding in the world will not be of help.

In contrast to the epic, which can describe human beings as they are, the drama unavoidably limits and therefore stylizes them. This limitation is inherent in the art form itself. The human being of the drama is, after all, a talking individual, and speech is his limitation. The action only serves to force this human being on the stage to talk in a certain way. The action is the crucible in which the human being is molten into words, must become words. This, of course, means that I, as the playwright, have to get the people in my drama into situations which force them to speak. If I merely show two people sitting together and drinking coffee while they talk about the weather, politics or the latest fashions, then I provide neither a dramatic situation nor dramatic dialogue, no matter how clever their talk. Some other ingredient must be added to their conversation, something to add pique, drama, double meaning. If the audience knows that there is some poison in one of the coffee cups, or perhaps even in both, so that the conversation is really one between two poisoners, then this little coffee-for-two idyll becomes through this artistic device a dramatic situation, out of which and on the basis of which dramatic dialogue can develop. Without the addition of some special tension or special condition, dramatic dialogue cannot develop.

Just as dialogue must develop out of a situation, so it must also lead into some situation, that is to say, of course, a new situation. Dramatic dialogue effects some action, some suffering, some new situation, out of which in turn new dialogue can again develop, and so on and so forth.

However, a human being does more than just talk. The fact that a man also thinks, or at least should think, that he feels, yes, more than anything feels, and that he does not always wish to show others what he is thinking or feeling, has led to the use of another artistic device, the monologue. It is true, of course, that a person standing on a stage and carrying on a conversation with himself out loud is not exactly natural; and the same thing can be said, only more so, of an operatic aria. But the monologue (like the aria) proves that an artistic trick, which really ought not to be played, can achieve an unexpected effect, to which, and rightly so, the public succumbs time and again; so much so that Hamlet's monologue, 'To be or not to be', or Faust's, are among the most beloved and most famous passages in the theatre.

But not everything that sounds like a monologue is monologue. The purpose of dialogue is not only to lead a human being to a point where he must act or suffer; at times it also leads into a major speech, to the explanation of some point of view. Many people have lost the appreciation of rhetoric since, as Hilpert maintains, some actor who was not sure of his lines discovered naturalism. That loss is rather sad. A speech can win its way across the footlights more effectively than any other artistic device. But many of our critics no longer know what to make of a speech. An author who today dares a speech will suffer the same fate as the peasant Dicaeopolis; he will have to lay his head upon the executioner's block. Except that instead of the Acharnians of Aristophanes, it will be the majority of critics who descend on the author – the most normal thing in the world. Nobody is more anxious to bash out someone's brains than those who haven't any.

Moreover, the drama has always embodied some narrative elements; epic drama did not introduce this. So, for instance, the background of an action has always had to be related, or an event announced in the form of a messenger's report. But narration on the stage is not without its dangers, for it does not live in the same manner, is not tangible the way an action taking place on the stage is. Attempts have been made to overcome this, as by dramatizing the messenger, by letting him appear at a crucial moment, or by making him a blockhead from whom a report can only be extracted with great difficulties. Yet certain elements of rhetoric must still be present if narration is to succeed on the stage. Stage narratives cannot exist without some exaggeration. Observe, for instance, how Shakespeare elaborates on Plutarch's description of Cleopatra's barge. This exaggeration is not just a characteristic of the baroque style, but a means of launching Cleopatra's barge upon the stage, of making it visible there. But while the speech of the theatre cannot exist without exaggeration, it is important to know when to exaggerate and above all, how.

Furthermore, just as stage characters can suffer a certain fate, so also can their language. The angel that came to Babylon, for example, grows more and more enthusiastic about the earth's beauty from act to act, and hence his language must parallel this rising enthusiasm until it grows into a veritable hymn. In the same comedy the beggar Akki relates his life in a series of *makamat*, passages of a rich and stately prose interspersed with rhymes, refined in grammar, rhetoric, poetic idiom and tradition, that come from the Arabic and flourished a thousand years ago. In this way I try to convey the Arabic character of this personage, his joy in inventing stories and in duelling and playing with words, without at the same time wandering off into another

24

form, the chanson. The *makamat* or anecdotes of Akki are nothing less than the most extreme possibilities offered by his language, and therefore they intensify his being. Through the *makamat* Akki has become all language, and this is just what an author must always strive for, so that there are moments in his plays in which the characters he has created with the written word become living language and nothing less.

A danger lurks here, too, of course. Language can lead a writer astray. The joy of being able all of a sudden to write, of possessing language, as it came over me, for instance, while I was writing *The Blind Man*, can make an author talk too much, can make him escape from his subject into language. To keep close to the subject is itself a great art, achieved only by masterful control of the impetus to talk. Dialogue, like playing on words, can also lead an author into byways, take him unawares away from his subject. Yet ideas flash into his mind again and again, ideas which he ought not resist, even if they disrupt his carefully laid plans. For in addition to being on guard against some of these tempting flashes of ideas, a writer must also have the courage to follow some of them.

These elements and problems of place, time, and action, which are all, of course, interwoven and are but hinted at here, belong to the basic material, to the artistic devices and tools of the craft of the drama. But let me make it clear here and now that I make war upon the notion of 'the craft of the drama'. The very idea that anyone who makes a sufficiently diligent and steadfast endeavour to achieve something in that art will succeed in the end, or even that this craft can be learned, is a notion we thought discarded long ago. Yet it is still frequently met with in critical writings about the art of play-writing. This art is supposed to be a sound and solid, respectable and well-mannered affair. Thus, too, the relationship between a playwright and his art is considered by some to be like a marriage in which everything is quite legal when blessed with the sacraments of aesthetics. For these reasons, perhaps, critics often refer to the theatre, much more than to any other form of art, as a craft which, depending on the particular case, has been more or less mastered. If we investigate closely what the critics really mean by 'the craft of the drama', then it becomes obvious that it is little else but the sum of their prejudices. There is no craft of the theatre; there is only the mastery of the material through language and the stage or, to be more exact, it is an overpowering of the material, for any creative writing is a kind of warfare with its victories, defeats and indecisive battles. Perfect plays do not exist except as a fiction of aesthetics in which, as in the films, perfect heroes may alone be found. Never yet has a playwright left this battle without his wounds; each one has his Achilles' heel, and the playwright's antagonist, his material, never fights fairly. It is cunning stuff, often not to be drawn out of its lair, and it employs highly secret and low-down tricks. This forces the playwright to fight back with every permissible and even non-permissible means, no matter what the wise exhortations, rules and adages of the masters of this craft and their most honoured trade may say. Best foot forward won't get an author anywhere in the drama, not even his foot in the doorway. The difficulties in writing for the drama lie where no one suspects them; sometimes it is no more than the problem of how to have two people say hello, or the difficulty in writing an opening sentence. What is sometimes considered to be the craft of the drama can be easily learned in half an hour. But how difficult it is to divide a given material into five acts, and how few subjects there are which can be divided that way, how nearly impossible it is to write today in iambic pentameter, those things are hardly ever suspected by the hack writers who can slap a play together any time and without trouble, who can always divide any subject into five acts, and who have always written and still write with facility in iambic pentameter. They really pick their material and their language in the way some critics think this is done. They are not so much amateurs when they talk about art as when they tailor art to their talk. No matter what the material is like, they always fashion the same bath-robe to be sure the audience will not catch cold and that it will sleep comfortably. There is nothing more idiotic than the opinion that only a genius does not have to obey those rules prescribed for writers of talent. In that case I should like to be counted among the geniuses. What I want to emphasize strongly is that the art of writing a play does not necessarily start out with the planning of a certain child, or however else a eunuch thinks love is made; but it starts out with love-making, of which a eunuch is incapable. Though really the difficulties, pains and also fortunes of writing do not lie within the realm of things we mean to talk about or even can talk about. We can only talk about the craft of the drama, a craft that exists only when one *talks* of drama, but not when one writes plays. The craft of the drama is an optical illusion. To talk about plays, about art, is a much more utopian undertaking than is ever appreciated by those who talk the most.

Employing this – really non-existent – craft, let us try and give shape to a certain material. Usually there is a central point of reference, the hero. In theories of the drama a difference is made between a tragic hero, the hero of tragedy, and a comic hero, the hero of comedy. The qualities a tragic hero must possess are well known. He must be capable of rousing our sympathy. His guilt and his innocence, his virtues and his vices must be mixed in the most pleasant and yet exact manner, and administered in doses according to well-defined rules. If, for example, I make my tragic hero an evil man, then I must endow him with a portion of intellect equal to his malevolence. As a result of this rule, the most sympathetic stage character in German literature has turned out to be the devil. The role of the hero in the play has not changed. The only thing that has changed is the social position of the character who awakens our sympathy.

In ancient tragedy and in Shakespeare the hero belongs to the highest class in society, to the nobility. The spectators watch a suffering, acting, raving hero who occupies a social position far higher than their own. This still continues to impress audiences today.

Then when Lessing and Schiller introduced the bourgeois drama, the audience saw itself as the suffering hero on the stage. But the evolution of the hero continued. Büchner's Wozzeck is a primitive proletarian who represents far less socially than the average spectator. But it is precisely in this extreme form of human existence, in this last, most miserable form, that the audience is to see the human being also, indeed itself.

And finally we might mention Pirandello who was the first, as far as I know, to render the hero, the character on the stage, immaterial and transparent just as Wilder did the dramatic place. The audience watching this sort of presentation attends, as it were, its own dissection, its own psycho-analysis, and the stage becomes man's internal milieu, the inner space of the world.

Of course, the theatre has never dealt only with kings and generals; in comedy the hero has always been the peasant, the beggar, the ordinary citizen – but this was always in comedy. Nowhere in Shakespeare do we find a comic king; in his day a ruler could appear as a bloody monster but never as a fool. In Shakespeare the courtiers, the artisans, the working people are comic. Hence, in the evolution of the tragic hero we see a trend towards comedy. Analogously the fool becomes more and more of a tragic figure. This fact is by no means without significance. The hero of a play not only propels an action on, he not only suffers a certain fate, but he also represents a world. Therefore we have to ask ourselves how we should present our own questionable world and with what sort of heroes. We have to ask ourselves how the mirrors which catch and reflect this world should be ground and set.

Can our present-day world, to ask a concrete question, be represented by Schiller's dramatic art? Some writers claim it can be, since Schiller still holds audiences in his grip. To be sure, in art everything is possible when the art is right. But the question is if an art valid for its time could possibly be so even for our day.

Art can never be repeated. If it were repeatable, it would be foolish not just to write according to the rules of Schiller.

Schiller wrote as he did because the world in which he lived could still be mirrored in the world his writing created, a world he could build as an historian. But just barely. For was not Napoleon perhaps the last hero in the old sense? The world today as it appears to us could hardly be encompassed in the form of the historical drama as Schiller wrote it, for the reason alone that we no longer have any tragic heroes, but only vast tragedies staged by world butchers and produced by slaughtering machines. Hitler and Stalin cannot be made into Wallensteins. Their power was so enormous that they themselves were no more than incidental, corporeal and easily replaceable expressions of this power; and the misfortune associated with the former and to a considerable extent also with the latter is too vast, too complex, too horrible, too mechanical and usually simply too devoid of all sense. Wallenstein's power can still be envisioned; power as we know it today can only be seen in its smallest part for, like an iceberg, the largest part is submerged in anonymity and abstraction. Schiller's drama presupposes a world that the eye can take in, that takes for granted genuine actions of state, just as Greek tragedy did. For only what the eye can take in can be made visible in art. The state today, however, cannot be envisioned, for it is anonymous and bureaucratic; and not only in Moscow and Washington, but also in Berne. Actions of state today have become *post-hoc* satyric dramas which follow the tragedies executed in secret earlier. True representatives of our world are missing; the tragic heroes are nameless. Any small-time crook, petty government official or policeman better represents our world than a senator or president. Today art can only embrace the victims, if it can reach men at all; it can no longer come close to the mighty. Creon's secretaries close Antigone's case. The state has lost its physical reality, and just as physics can now only cope with the world in mathematical formulae, so the state can only be expressed in statistics. Power today becomes visible, material only when it explodes as in the atom bomb, in this marvellous mushroom which rises and spreads immaculate as the sun and in which mass murder and beauty have become one. The atom bomb cannot be reproduced artistically since it is mass-produced. In its face all man's art that would recreate it must fail, since it is itself a creation of man. Two mirrors which reflect one another remain empty.

But the task of art, in so far as art can have a task at all, and hence also the task of drama today, is to create something concrete, something that has form. This can be accomplished best by comedy. Tragedy, the strictest genre in art, presupposes a formed world. Comedy – in so far as it is not just satire of a particular society as in Molière – supposes an unformed world, a world being made and turned upside down, a world about to fold like ours. Tragedy overcomes distance; it can make myths originating in times immemorial seem like the present to the Athenians. But comedy creates distance; the attempt of the Athenians to gain a foothold in Sicily is translated by comedy into the birds undertaking to create their own empire before which the gods and men will have to capitulate. How comedy works can be seen in the most primitive kind of joke, in the dirty story, which, though it is of very dubious value, I bring up only because it is the best illustration of what I mean by creating distance. The subject of the dirty story is the purely sexual, which because it is purely sexual, is formless and without objective distance. To give form the purely sexual is transmuted, as I have already mentioned, into the dirty joke. Therefore this type of joke is a kind of original comedy, a transposition of the sexual on to the plain of the comical. In this way it is possible today, in a society dominated by John Doe, to talk in an accepted way about the purely sexual. In the dirty story it becomes clear that the comical exists in forming what is formless, in creating order out of chaos.

The means by which comedy creates distance is the conceit.

Tragedy is without conceit. Hence there are few tragedies whose subjects were invented. By this I do not mean to imply that the ancient tragedians lacked inventive ideas of the sort that are written today, but the marvel of their art was that they had no need of these inventions, of conceits. That makes all the difference. Aristophanes, on the other hand, lives by conceits. The stuff of his plays are not myths but inventions, which take place not in the past but the present. They drop into their world like bomb-shells which, by throwing up huge craters of dirt, change the present into the comic and thus scatter the dirt for everyone to see. This, of course, does not mean that drama today can only be comical. Tragedy and comedy are but formal concepts, dramatic attitudes, figments of the aesthetic imagination which can embrace one and the same thing. Only the conditions under which each is created are different, and these conditions have their basis only in small part in art.

Tragedy presupposes guilt, despair, moderation, lucidity, vision, a sense of responsibility. In the Punch-and-Judy show of our century, in this back-sliding of the white race, there are no more guilty and also, no responsible men. It is always, 'We couldn't help it' and 'We didn't really want that to happen.' And indeed, things happen without anyone in particular being responsible for them. Everything is dragged along and everyone gets caught somewhere in the sweep of events. We are all collectively guilty, collectively bogged down in the sins of our fathers and of our forefathers. We are the offspring of children. That is our misfortune, but not our guilt: guilt can exist only as a personal achievement, as a religious deed. Comedy alone is suitable for us. Our world has led to the grotesque as well as to the atom bomb, and so it is a world like that of Hieronymus Bosch whose apocalyptic paintings are also grotesque. But the grotesque is only a way of expressing in a tangible manner, of making us perceive physically the paradoxical, the form of the unformed, the face of a world without face; and just as in our thinking today we seem to be unable to do without the concept of the paradox, so also in art, and in our world which at times seems still to exist only because the atom bomb exists: out of fear of the bomb.

But the tragic is still possible even if pure tragedy is not. We can achieve the tragic out of comedy. We can bring it forth as a frightening moment, as an abyss that opens suddenly; indeed, many of Shakespeare's tragedies are already really comedies out of which the tragic arises.

After all this the conclusion might easily be drawn that comedy is the expression of despair, but this conclusion is not inevitable. To be sure, whoever realizes the senselessness, the hopelessness of this world might well despair, but this despair is not a result of this world. Rather it is an answer given by an individual to this world; another answer would be not to despair, would be an individual's decision to endure this world in which we live like Gulliver among the giants. He also achieves distance, he also steps back a pace or two who takes measure of his opponent, who prepares himself to fight his opponent or to escape him. It is still possible to show man as a courageous being.

In truth this is a principal concern of mine. The blind man, Romulus, Übelohe, Akki, are all men of courage. The lost world-order is restored within them; the universal escapes my grasp. I refuse to find the universal in a doctrine. The universal for me is chaos. The world (hence the stage which represents this world) is for me something monstrous, a riddle of misfortunes which must be accepted but before which one must not capitulate. The world is far bigger than any man, and perforce threatens him constantly. If one could but stand outside the world, it would no longer be threatening. But I have neither the right nor the ability to be an outsider to this world. To find solace in poetry can also be all too cheap; it is more honest to retain one's human point of view. Brecht's thesis, that the world is an accident, which he developed in his *Street Scene* where he shows how this accident happened, may yield – as it in fact did – some magnificent theatre; but he did it by concealing most of the evidence!

Brecht's thinking is inexorable, because inexorably there are many things he will not think about.

And lastly it is through the conceit, through comedy, that the anonymous audience becomes possible as an audience, becomes a reality to be counted on, and also one to be taken into account. The conceit easily transforms the crowd of theatre-goers into a mass which can be attacked, deceived, outsmarted into listening to things it would otherwise not so readily listen to. Comedy is a mouse-trap in which the public is easily caught and in which it will get caught over and over again. Tragedy, on the other hand, predicated a true community, a kind of community whose existence in our day is but an embarrassing fiction. Nothing is more ludicrous, for instance, than to sit and watch the mystery plays of the Anthroposophists when one is not a participant.

Granting all this, there is still one more question to be asked: is it permissible to go from a generality to a particular form of art, to do what I just did when I went from my assertion that the world was formless to the particular possibility for writing comedies today. I doubt that this is permissible. Art is something personal, and something personal should never be explained with generalities. The value of a work of art does not depend on whether more or less good reasons for its existence can be found. Hence I have also tried to avoid certain problems, as for example the argument which is quite lively today, whether or not plays ought to be written in verse or in prose. My own answer lies simply in writing prose, without any intention of thereby deciding the issue. A man has to choose to go one way, after all, and why should one way always be worse than another? As far as my concepts of comedy are concerned, I believe that here, too, personal reasons are more important than more general ones that are always open to argument. What logic in matters of art could not be refuted! One talks best about art when one talks of one's own art. The art one chooses is an expression of freedom without which no art can exist, and at the same time also of necessity without which art

33

cannot exist either. The artist always represents his world and himself. If at one time philosophy taught men to arrive at the particular from the general, then – unlike Schiller, who started out believing in general conclusions – I cannot construct a play as he did when I doubt that the particular can ever be reached from the general. But my doubt is mine and only mine, and not the doubt and problems of a Catholic for whom drama holds possibilities non-Catholics do not share. This is so even if, on the other hand, a Catholic who takes his religion seriously, is denied those possibilities which other men possess. The danger inherent in this thesis lies in the fact that there are always those artists who for the sake of finding some generalities to believe in accept conversion, taking a step which is the more to be wondered at for the sad fact that it really will not help them. The difficulties experienced by a Protestant in writing a drama are just the same difficulties he has with his faith. Thus it is my way to mistrust what is ordinarily called the building of the drama, and to arrive at my plays from the unique, the sudden idea or conceit, rather than from some general concept or plan. Speaking for myself, I need to write off into the blue, as I like to put it so that I might give critics a catchword to hang on to. They use it often enough, too, without really understanding what I mean by it.

But these matters are my own concerns and hence it is not necessary to invoke the whole world and to make out that what are my concerns are the concerns of art in general (lest I be like the drunk who goes back to Noah, the Flood, original sin and the beginning of the world to explain what is, after all, only his own weakness). As in everything and everywhere, and not just in the field of art, the rule is: No excuses, please!

Nevertheless the fact remains (always keeping in mind, of course, the reservations just made) that we now stand in a different relationship to what we have called our material. Our unformed, amorphous present is characterized by being surrounded by figures and forms that reduce our time to a mere result, even less, to a mere transitional state, and which give excessive weight to the past as something finished and to the future as something possible. This applies equally well to politics. Related to art it means that the artist is surrounded by all sort of opinions about art and by demands on him which are based not upon his capacities, but upon the historical past and present forms. He is surrounded therefore by materials which are no longer materials, that is possibilities, but by materials which have already taken on shape, that is some definitive form. Caesar is no longer pure subject matter for us; he has become the Caesar whom scholarship made the object of its researches. And so it happened that scholars, having thrown themselves with increasing energy not only upon nature but also upon intellectual life and upon art, establishing in the process intellectual history, literary scholarship, philology and goodness knows what else, have created a body of factual information which cannot be ignored (for one cannot be conscious of these facts and at the same time pretend to be so naïve that one need pay no attention to the results of scholarship). In this way, however, scholars have deprived the artist of materials by doing what was really the artist's task. The mastery of Richard Feller's *History of Berne* precludes the possibility of an historical drama about the city of Berne; the history of Berne was thus given shape before some literary artist could do it. True, it is a scholastic form (and not a mythical one which would leave the way open for a tragedian), a form that severely limits the field for the artist, leaving to art only psychology which, of course, has also become a science. To rewrite such a history in a creative literary manner would now be a tautology, a repetition by means which are not suitable or fitting, a mere illustration of scholarly insights; in short, it would be the very thing science often claims literature to be. It was still possible for Shakespeare to base his Caesar upon Plutarch, for the Roman was not an historian in our sense of the word but a story-teller, the author of biographical sketches. Had Shakespeare read Mommsen he could not have written his Caesar because he would of necessity

35

have lost the supremacy over his materials. And this holds true now in all things, even the myths of the Greeks which, since we no longer live them but only study, evaluate, investigate them, recognizing them to be mere myths and as such destroying them, have become mummies; and these, bound tightly round with philosophy and theology, are all too often substituted for the living thing.

Therefore the artist must reduce the subjects he finds and runs into everywhere if he wants to turn them once more into real materials, hoping always that he will succeed. He parodies his materials, contrasts them consciously with what they have actually been turned into. By this means, by this act of parody, the artist regains his freedom and hence his material; and thus material is no longer found but invented. For every parody presupposes a conceit and an invention. In laughter man's freedom becomes manifest, in crying his necessity. Our task today is to demonstrate freedom. The tyrants of this planet are not moved by the works of the poets. They yawn at a poet's threnodies. For them heroic epics are silly fairy-tales and religious poetry puts them to sleep. Tyrants fear only one thing: a poet's mockery. For this reason, then, parody has crept into all literary genres, into the novel, the drama, into lyrical poetry. Much of painting, even of music, has been conquered by parody, and the grotesque has followed, often well camouflaged, on the heels of parody: all of a sudden the grotesque is there.

But our times, up to every imaginable trick there is, can handle all that and nothing can intimidate it: the public has been educated to see in art something solemn, hallowed and even pathetic. The comic is considered inferior, dubious, unseemly; it is accepted only when it makes people feel as bestially happy as a bunch of pigs. But the very moment people recognize the comic to be dangerous, an art that exposes, demands, moralizes, it is dropped like a hot potato, for art may be everything it wants to be so long as it remains *gemütlich*.

36

We writers are often accused of art that is nihilistic. Today, of course, there exists a nihilistic art, but not every art that seems nihilistic is so. True nihilistic art does not appear to be nihilistic at all; usually it is considered to be especially humane and supremely worthy of being read by our more mature young people. A man must be a pretty bungling sort of nihilist to be recognized as such by the world at large. People call nihilistic what is merely uncomfortable. Then also people say, the artist is supposed to create, not to talk; to give shape to things, not to preach. To be sure. But it becomes more and more difficult to create 'purely' or however people imagine the creative mind should work. Mankind today is like a reckless driver racing ever faster, ever more heedlessly along the highway. And he does not like it when the frightened passengers cry out, 'Watch out' and 'There's a warning sign! Slow down', or 'Don't kill that child!' What is more, the driver hates it even worse when he is asked, 'Who is paying for the car?' or 'Who's providing the petrol and oil for this mad journey?', to say nothing of what happens when he is asked for his driver's licence. What unpleasant facts might then come to light! Maybe the car was stolen from some relatives, the petrol and oil squeezed from the passengers, and really not petrol and oil but the blood and sweat of us all; and most likely he wouldn't even have a driver's licence and it would turn out that this was his first time driving. Of course, it would be embarrassing if such personal questions were to be asked. The driver would much prefer the passengers to praise the beauty of the countryside through which they are travelling, the silver of the river and the brilliant reflection of the ice-capped mountains in the far distance, would even prefer to have amusing stories whispered into his ear. Today's author, however, can no longer confine himself with good conscience to whispering pleasant stories and praising the beautiful landscape. Unfortunately, too, he cannot get out of this mad race in order to sit by the wayside, writing the pure poetry demanded of him by all the non-poets. Fear, worry, and above all anger open his mouth wide.

How very nice it would be if we could end now on this emphatic note. It would be a conclusion that could be considered at least partially safe and not wholly impossible. But in all honesty we must ask ourselves at this point if any of this makes sense today, if it were not better if we practised silence. I have tried to show that the theatre today is, in the best sense of the word to be sure, in part a museum, and in part a field of experimentation. I have also tried to show here and there what these experiments are. Is the theatre capable of fulfilling this, its latter destiny? Not only has the writing of plays become more difficult today but also the rehearsing and performing of these plays is harder. The very lack of time results at best in only a decent attempt, a first probing, a slight advance in what might be the right direction. A play that is to be more than a merely conventional piece, that is really to be an experiment, can no longer be solved at the writing desk. Giraudoux's fortune was that he had Jouvet. Unhappily this happens only once or twice. The repertory theatre of Germany can afford less and less to experiment. A new play must be got rid of as quickly as possible. The museum's treasures weigh too heavily in the scales. The theatre, our whole culture, lives on the interest of the well invested intellect, to which nothing can happen any more and for which not even royalties have to be paid. Assured of having a Goethe, Schiller or Sophocles at hand, the theatres are willing now and then to put on a modern piece – but preferably only for a premiere performance. Heroically this duty is discharged, and sighs of relief are breathed all round when Shakespeare is performed next time. What can we say or do? Clear the stages completely! Make room for the classics! The world of the museum is growing and bursts with its treasures. The cultures of the cave-dwellers have not yet been investigated to the nth degree. Let the custodians of the future concern themselves with our art when it is our turn. It does not make much difference then if something new is added, something new is written. The demands made of the artist by aesthetics increase from day to day. What is wanted is the perfection which is read into the classics. And let the artist even be suspected of having taken one step backwards, of having made a mistake, just watch how quickly he is dropped. Thus a climate is created in which literature can be studied but not made. How can the artist exist in a world of educated and literate people? This question oppresses me, and I know no answer. Perhaps the writer can best exist by writing detective stories, by creating art where it is least suspected. Literature must become so light that it will weigh nothing upon the scale of today's literary criticism: only in this way will it regain its true worth.

[This version of *Problems of the Theatre* was prepared for publication from the manuscript of a lecture delivered by Friedrich Dürrenmatt in the autumn of 1954 and the spring of 1955 in different cities of Switzerland and West Germany.]

THE MARRIAGE OF
MR. MISSISSIPPI

TRANSLATED FROM THE GERMAN
BY MICHAEL BULLOCK

CHARACTERS

ANASTASIA
FLORESTAN MISSISSIPPI
FRÉDÉRIC RENÉ SAINT-CLAUDE
COUNT BODO VON ÜBELOHE-ZABERNSEE
DIEGO, the Minister of Justice
THE MAID
THREE PRIESTS
THREE MEN in raincoats with their right hands in their pockets
TWO WARDERS
PROFESSOR ÜBERHUBER
PSYCHIATRISTS

PART ONE

A room whose late-bourgeois magnificence and splendour will not be altogether easy to describe. Yet since the action takes place in this room and in this room alone, since in fact we may say that the events which follow represent the story of this room, an attempt must be made to describe it. The room stinks to high heaven. In the background are two windows. The view from them is bewildering. To the right the branches of an apple tree, and behind it some northern city with a Gothic cathedral; to the left a cypress, the remains of a classical temple, a bay, a harbour. So much for what lies outside. Between the two windows, but no higher than they are, a grandfather clock. Also Gothic in style. Let us turn to the right-hand wall. Here there are two doors. The door at the back of the stage leads through the veranda into a second room – it isn't important, I really only need it in Part Two; the door front stage right leads to an entrance hall and the front door; the kitchen is also situated there, perhaps round the corner to the right of the entrance hall. Let us not bother about the possible lay-out of the house, we will assume that it is a rambling mansion to which many alterations and additions have been made. Between the doors on the right stands a small sideboard; this time I should like to suggest Louis Quinze. On it is a Venus. Of plaster. Naturally. In the left-hand wall there is only one door. It opens between fin-de-siècle mirrors. The door leads into a boudoir, which in turn leads into the bedroom, rooms which we shall not enter – though many others will. Front stage left the Louis Seize frame of a second mirror dangles in mid-air, of course without a glass, so that anyone looking in it will see the audience. Front stage right there might hang a small, oval, blank picture. In the centre stands a round Biedermeier coffee table; this is really the main character in the play, upon which all the action centres, and the production should make this clear; it is flanked by

45

two Louis Quatorze chairs. A bit of Empire furniture can undoubtedly be introduced somewhere – say, left front stage a small sofa and left back stage a folding screen. The producer will have to forgo putting in anything Russian, unless the political situation happens to render this desirable. On the little table stands a Japanese vase containing red roses in Part One. I suggest that Part Two should take place without flowers. The table is laid for coffee for three people. One guesses it is Dresden china. Further objects: to the right three MEN, *looking not unlike good-humoured brewers, wearing raincoats and red armbands, their right hands in their pockets; and in the centre, say between the coffee table and the door on the left, or perhaps slightly to the south of the latter,* SAINT-CLAUDE. *Without going into great detail regarding this character we may think of him as rather squarely built, massive, a man of steel, dressed at the moment in evening dress that obviously doesn't fit, and red socks. In addition, somewhere in the room, preferably coming from the cathedral, the solemn ringing of bells.*

THE FIRST OF THE THREE IN RAINCOATS. You have been condemned to death, Saint-Claude. Put your hands behind your head.

(SAINT-CLAUDE *obeys.*)

Go and stand between the windows.

(SAINT-CLAUDE *obeys.*)

Turn your face to the wall. That's the simplest way to die.

(SAINT-CLAUDE *turns his face to the wall. The ringing dies away. A shot.* SAINT-CLAUDE *stands where he is. The three* MEN *in raincoats – their right hands in their pockets again – go out right.* SAINT-CLAUDE *turns round to the audience and delivers the following speech, like a cross between the director of a rather second-rate theatre and a Mephistopheles.*)

SAINT-CLAUDE. Ladies and gentlemen, as you may have noticed, I have just been shot to the sound of church bells fading into the distance. The bullet struck me somewhere between the

46

shoulder blades, as far as I can judge – it's not easy to be sure – (*he reaches round to feel his back*) shattered my heart on its way through and apparently came out of my chest here, making a hole in my tail coat and buckling the medal 'Pour le Mérite' – which is a bit embarrassing, since neither the coat nor the medal belong to me – and finally damaging the wallpaper. At least, that is what I imagine happened. My present condition is a pleasant one. Apart from my very natural surprise at finding myself still here, I feel fine; in particular, my liver has suddenly ceased to bother me. It used to be the seat of an insidious disease which in my life before death I was always trying to conceal, but which, as I must now admit, was largely responsible for my rather extreme views – although at the time I thought I was governed solely by moral considerations. My death, which you have just witnessed – this exceedingly trivial but, sad to relate, not by any means unusual death – really takes place at the end of the play, as you may have guessed, because once men with armbands appear on the scene the game's up, it's the end of everything. But for what I might call therapeutic reasons we have shifted my murder to the beginning; this enables us to get one of the worst scenes over quickly. Moreover – and I can't hide this from you either – at the painful moment when my death takes place there will be other bodies lying around here, a fact which at this juncture would only confuse you, although it is not really surprising, since this comedy deals, among other things, with the marriage of my friend Mr Mississippi. Among other things, I say, because it concerns the somewhat regrettable fate of three men (*three over-dramatic busts, portraying from left to right Saint-Claude, Übelohe and Mississippi, the two outside ones encircled by black crape, descend from above and remain suspended in the air back stage*) who, for various reasons, had taken it into their heads to change and save the world and who then had the appalling bad luck to run into a woman (*Anastasia's bust descends, likewise encircled by black crape, and remains suspended between Übelohe and Mississippi*) who could be neither changed nor saved, because she loved nothing but the moment; though looking back on it I must say that this is by far the pleasantest attitude to adopt to life. Anyhow, this comedy might just as well have been called 'The Love of Bodo von Übelohe-Zabernsee', or 'The Adventure of Monsieur Saint-Claude' or, to keep it short and sweet, 'Anastasia and her Lovers'. (*As he speaks he points in turn to the character concerned.*) The fact that as the plot develops every project finally comes to nothing, indeed that the whole thing degenerates into violence and confusion, is regrettable, but that is life, and in any case it is too late to change it now. (*The busts disappear.*) And if at this moment you see one of the few survivors staggering past outside the two windows – look, there he goes – (COUNT ÜBELOHE *staggers past outside with a blue banner*) running after some ridiculous detachment of the Salvation Army, banner in hand, please overlook the fact that this is completely impossible, since this room is on the first floor, as may be gathered from the tops of the two trees which you can see – an apple tree and a cypress, to be precise. But let's make some sort of start with our story. We might begin, for example, with myself in Rumania hatching up the revolution that led to the fall of King Michael, or with Count Übelohe in Tampang, a miserable dump in the interior of Borneo, trying to cut out a drunken Malay's appendix while drunk himself (*two pictures showing what is being described float down from above*), but let us remain in this room that has now grown familiar to us. Let us go back (*the pictures float upwards again*); we shall not find that difficult, since we need not move from the spot – though it isn't even clear where this house is situated; at one point the author decided in favour of the south, hence the cypress, the temple and the sea; at another, he settled for the north, hence the apple tree and the cathedral. Anyhow, let us go back, if you please, just five years before the disaster which you witnessed at the beginning, back in other words to 1958 or 1959, always five years before the present, so long as this remains possible at all. Well, then, it is May, the windows are slightly open (*the windows open slightly*), on the table stand red roses, above the grandfather clock hangs the portrait of the first man who had the good fortune to be married to Anastasia, the picture of a beet-sugar manufacturer whose Christian name was François (*the picture floats down*), and the maid brings in my old friend Mississippi (*the* MAID *and* MISSISSIPPI *enter right*), who stands there, correct as always and dressed as always in a black frock-coat, and hands his stick, coat and hat to the girl, while I make off in my usual way – I climbed through windows far too often in my previous life; in fact this may not be the normal manner for the dead to disappear, but how could I be expected to have learnt their trick of fading into thin air all on my own, when I was scarcely cold? In short, while I am making for a place (*he looks somewhat suspiciously towards the centre of the earth*) which I can't picture to myself at all (*he climbs through the window left*), Mr Mississippi, five years ago and at this particular spot, reaches an important decision.

(SAINT-CLAUDE *disappears.*)

THE MAID. Madam will be here in a moment, sir.

(*The* MAID *goes out right,* MISSISSIPPI *looks at the beet-sugar manufacturer's picture.* ANASTASIA *enters left.* MISSISSIPPI *bows.*)

ANASTASIA. You wished to see me?

MISSISSIPPI. My name is Mississippi. Florestan Mississippi.

ANASTASIA. You told me in your letter that you had an urgent matter to discuss with me?

MISSISSIPPI. Yes, very urgent. I'm afraid my work prevents me from coming at any other time than in my lunch hour.

ANASTASIA. You were a friend of my husband's?

(*She glances briefly at the picture in the background.* MISSISSIPPI *also looks at it.*)

MISSISSIPPI. I am deeply affected by his unexpected death.

(*He bows.*)

49

ANASTASIA (*somewhat embarrassed*). He died of a heart attack.

MISSISSIPPI (*bows again*). May I express my profound sympathy?

ANASTASIA. May I offer you a cup of coffee?

MISSISSIPPI. You are very kind.

(*They sit down.* ANASTASIA *on the left,* MISSISSIPPI *on the right.* ANASTASIA *pours out. The ensuing scene at the coffee table must be produced with great exactitude, the movements involved in drinking coffee being performed very precisely: e.g. both lift their cups to their mouths at the same time or stir the coffee simultaneously etc.*)

ANASTASIA. In your letter you urgently begged me to hear what you had to say. You did so in the name of my dead husband. (*She looks at the picture.*) Otherwise I should not have agreed to your visit so soon after François's death. I hope you understand me.

MISSISSIPPI. Perfectly. I too honour the dead. (*He too looks at the picture.*) Were my business not so urgent I should never have ventured to inflict my visit upon you, all the more so since there has also been a death in my family. My young wife died a few days ago. (*After a short pause, meaningfully.*) Her name was Madeleine.

(*He looks searchingly at* ANASTASIA, *who has almost imperceptibly started.*)

ANASTASIA. I'm sorry to hear that.

MISSISSIPPI. For years we had the same family doctor as you, old Dr Bonsels. It was from him that I heard the sad news of your husband's death. Dr Bonsels diagnosed heart failure as the cause of death in my wife's case too.

(*Again he looks watchfully at* ANASTASIA, *who once more starts.*)

ANASTASIA. May I too offer my heartfelt condolences?

MISSISSIPPI. In order to understand the request I am about to make it is most important that you should know all about me, Madam. I am the Public Prosecutor.

(ANASTASIA *drops her coffee cup in terror.*)

ANASTASIA. Forgive my clumsy interruption.

MISSISSIPPI (*bows*). Don't mention it. I am used to spreading fear and trembling.

(ANASTASIA *rings a small silver bell. The* MAID *enters right, mops the table, gives* ANASTASIA *a fresh cup and saucer and leaves again.*)

ANASTASIA. You haven't taken any sugar yet. Please help yourself.

MISSISSIPPI. Thank you.

ANASTASIA (*smiling*). What brings you to me now, Mr Public Prosecutor?

MISSISSIPPI. The reason for my visit concerns your husband.

ANASTASIA. Does François owe you money?

MISSISSIPPI. His debt is not of a financial character. We are totally unknown to one another, Madam, and I am sincerely sorry to have to speak ill of your husband, but he deceived you.

(ANASTASIA *starts and there is an awkward silence.*)

ANASTASIA (*coldly*). Who told you that?

MISSISSIPPI (*calmly*). My incorruptible powers of observation. I possess the ability to sniff out evil wherever it may be. It is a gift that causes me unimaginable suffering.

ANASTASIA. I really don't know how you can make such insane assertions about my husband's way of life so soon after his death and in this room, in which, so to speak, he still lives. Your accusation is monstrous.

MISSISSIPPI. The fact that your husband could deceive a woman such as you is a great deal more monstrous. Does it not occur to you that I have not come to you of my own free will, but only because we are bound together by an awful destiny? I beg you to steel your heart and listen to me calmly. Our mutual torment is already so dreadful that we must treat one another with the utmost consideration.

ANASTASIA (*after a brief pause, in a matter-of-fact tone*). Forgive my understandable agitation. François's unexpected death has exhausted my strength. Will you have another cup of coffee?

MISSISSIPPI. I should like one very much. My profession calls for iron nerves.

(*She pours out.*)

ANASTASIA. May I give you some sugar?

MISSISSIPPI. Thank you. Sugar has a calming effect. Unfortunately I am not in a position to set aside more than half an hour for our important discussion. I have to get a death sentence passed by a jury later this afternoon. Juries are very narrow-minded nowadays. (*He drinks coffee.*) So you still cling to the belief that your husband did not deceive you?

ANASTASIA. I swear that he is innocent.

MISSISSIPPI (*after a short pause*). Very well. You boast of his innocence. Will you continue to do so if I tell you the name of the woman with whom your husband deceived you?

ANASTASIA (*jumps up*). Who is this woman?

MISSISSIPPI (*after a short pause*). I have told you her name – Madeleine.

ANASTASIA (*horrified, because she has suddenly understood*). Your wife?

MISSISSIPPI. My wife.

ANASTASIA (*filled with horror*). But I thought she was dead?

MISSISSIPPI (*with the greatest possible calm*). Indeed she is. She died of heart failure. (*With dignity.*) We have been deceived by your husband François and my dead wife Madeleine, Madam.

ANASTASIA. It's terrible!

MISSISSIPPI. The facts of marriage are often terrible. (*He wipes the sweat from his brow with a handkerchief.*) Might I ask for another cup of coffee?

ANASTASIA (*crushed*). Please forgive me. I am upset and confused. (*She pours out.*)

MISSISSIPPI (*with relief*). The first stage of our terrible journey is behind us! You have confessed to knowing of your husband's infidelity. That is a tremendous step forward. Have you had proof for long?

ANASTASIA (*tonelessly*). For a few weeks. When I found a letter signed 'Madeleine' and filled with outpourings of the most ardent passion, the discovery stunned me like a blow from a club. I shall never understand my husband's action.

MISSISSIPPI. You didn't know my wife. She was the most lovable of women, young, radiantly beautiful and of medium height. The discovery of her infidelity cast me into the bottommost hell. I too found a letter imprudently headed with your husband's business address. Their love was already so wildly ablaze that they failed to take the most elementary precautions.

ANASTASIA. After my husband's death I wanted to forget his infidelity. I wanted to preserve the memory of him as the man who once loved me passionately and whom I shall never cease to love. That was why at first I evaded your question. I'm sorry. You have forced me to think once more about what has happened.

MISSISSIPPI. As the husband of the woman with whom your husband deceived you I'm afraid I couldn't possibly avoid it.

ANASTASIA. I too understand you. Being a man, you need clarity. (*She stands up.*) Thank you, Mr Public Prosecutor, for having given clarity to me too, weak woman that I am. Now I know all about François, and it is terrible to know all. (*Exhausted.*) Now you must excuse me, I am worn out. Your wife and my husband are dead. We can no longer call them to account. We can no longer beg them for love. They are now lost to us for ever.

(MISSISSIPPI *has now also risen.*)

MISSISSIPPI (*gravely*). At this unprecedented moment, when the first rays of truth are beginning to touch us, my twenty-five years as Public Prosecutor make it incumbent upon me to cry out to you that the time has come for us both to confess the whole truth, even if it destroys us.

(*He looks at her so resolutely that they sit down again.*)

ANASTASIA. I don't understand you.

MISSISSIPPI. I am referring to your husband's death.

ANASTASIA. I really don't know what you're getting at.

MISSISSIPPI. The fact that at the very beginning of our conversation, and for absolutely no apparent reason, you informed me of the cause of your husband's death, and your panic terror when I told you my profession, were all the evidence I needed.

ANASTASIA. Will you please be more explicit?

MISSISSIPPI. If you wish me to, I shall be utterly explicit. I doubt the cause of his death.

ANASTASIA (*quickly*). Many people die of a heart attack at the age of fifty.

MISSISSIPPI. His photograph alone disproves that. No man who enjoys such glowing health can die of a heart attack. Besides, people in whom I am interested never die of heart attacks.

ANASTASIA. What do you mean by that?

MISSISSIPPI. Could you really not have spared me the necessity of telling you to your face that you poisoned your husband?

ANASTASIA (*staring at him flabbergasted*). You believe that?

MISSISSIPPI (*distinctly*). I do.

ANASTASIA (*still as though stunned*). No, no!

(*She is deathly pale.* MISSISSIPPI *wearily takes a rose from the Japanese vase and holds it to his nose.*)

MISSISSIPPI. Get a grip on yourself. It must be something of a relief to you to have been found out by Justice.

ANASTASIA (*in a wild outburst*). No!

(MISSISSIPPI *replaces the rose in the vase.* ANASTASIA *rises to her feet with dignity.* MISSISSIPPI *does the same.*)

ANASTASIA. The physician, Dr Bonsels, had no hesitation in diagnosing the cause of my husband's death as heart failure. I presume that the Public Prosecutor will accept the verdict of medical science.

MISSISSIPPI. We belong to a social stratum, Madam, in which in cases of doubt medical science always diagnoses heart failure.

ANASTASIA. Now that I have told you everything that remained to be said regarding my husband's death, which came as a surprise to all of us, may I ask you to take your leave?

MISSISSIPPI (*worried*). In that terrible event it would be my duty to continue our discussion in a different room and under different circumstances.

ANASTASIA. I cannot prevent you from doing your so-called duty.

MISSISSIPPI. You can, if you take an unprejudiced view of your situation. You have the rare opportunity of confronting the Public Prosecutor between your own four walls. Do you wish to do so under the humiliating conditions of a Public Court? I hope not. I am altogether at a loss to understand why you refuse so disastrously to see the humanitarian nature of what I am doing. It is undoubtedly far easier to confess to a murder over coffee than before a jury.

(*They sit down again.*)

ANASTASIA (*in a low voice*). I am at your service.

MISSISSIPPI (*relieved*). That is unquestionably the best way.

ANASTASIA. But no power in the world will compel me to confess to the crime which you impute to me. You seem to be the victim of some terrible mistake.

MISSISSIPPI. Only the accused make mistakes, never the Public Prosecutor.

ANASTASIA. I shall defend my innocence like a wild beast.

MISSISSIPPI (*earnestly*). Pray to God, Madam, that you are spared such a fight. It is sheer madness to fight against me, and yet people are for ever trying to do so. For minutes, for hours, for days; then they break down. I shudder at the sight of my victims. Do you too wish to wriggle at my feet like a worm? Please realize that behind me stands the whole moral order of the universe, and that anyone who opposes me is lost. To confess may be difficult, but to be forced to confess is unimaginably frightful.

ANASTASIA. Are you a preacher or an executioner?

MISSISSIPPI. My terrible profession compels me to be both.

ANASTASIA. You can't come here and make the wildest accusations against me completely out of the blue like that.

MISSISSIPPI. Then I am afraid I must mention the name of Count Bodo von Übelohe-Zabernsee.

(ANASTASIA *is seized with fright, but recovers her poise.*)

ANASTASIA (*slowly*). I don't know that name.

MISSISSIPPI. You spent your youth with Count Übelohe in Lausanne, where your father was a teacher at a girls' boarding-school, and you grew up in a castle belonging to the Count's family. You parted, and a few years ago you met again in this town, you as the wife of your now dead husband and he as the head physician and founder of the St George's Hospital for the Poor.

ANASTASIA (*slowly*). I only see him very occasionally now.

MISSISSIPPI. On the sixteenth you asked him for two pieces of a white poison which looks exactly like sugar and about which he talked to you after you had been together to see *Götz von Berlichingen* and you came to speak of Weislingen's death. You are both great lovers of literature.

ANASTASIA (*stubbornly*). He didn't give me the poison.

MISSISSIPPI. Bodo von Übelohe-Zabernsee has confessed to everything.

ANASTASIA (*vehemently*). That's not true!

MISSISSIPPI. After I threatened to have his medical licence withdrawn he left our town as fast as he could and went to the tropics, no doubt to escape imprisonment.

ANASTASIA (*jumps up*). Bodo has gone?

MISSISSIPPI. The Count has fled.

(ANASTASIA *sinks back into the chair again.* MISSISSIPPI *wipes the sweat from his brow.*)

ANASTASIA (*after a long pause, dully*). Why did you threaten him with such a cruel step? The St George's Hospital for the Poor is his life's work.

MISSISSIPPI. I only acted according to the laws which govern the medical profession. (*After a short pause.*) According to the statement which he made when driven to utter despair, you told him that you wanted the poison in order to kill your dog, a statement which, of course, in no way excuses his giving it to you.

ANASTASIA (*quickly*). I did have to kill my dog. He was ill.

MISSISSIPPI (*politely*). You must permit me a brief incursion into your domestic rights.

(*He stands up, bows and rings* ANASTASIA's *little silver bell. The* MAID *enters right.*)

MISSISSIPPI. What is your name?

MAID. Lucretia.

MISSISSIPPI. Has your mistress a dog, Lucretia?

MAID. He's dead.

MISSISSIPPI. When did the dog die, Lucretia?

MAID. A month ago.

MISSISSIPPI. You may go back to work, Lucretia.

(*The* MAID *goes out right.* MISSISSIPPI *stands up.*)

MISSISSIPPI. You lost your dog a month ago and you fetched the poison from your childhood friend Count Übelohe-Zabernsee five days ago. Two pieces of a quick-acting poison that looked like lumps of sugar. Your husband died the same day. How much longer are we to keep up this comedy that is degrading for both of us, Madam? You force me to stoop to methods which a Public Prosecutor employs only reluctantly. Now I have even had to question your maid.

(ANASTASIA *also rises. At this point a little dance round the coffee table may be executed in the heat of the duel.*)

ANASTASIA (*in a low voice*). I didn't poison my husband.

MISSISSIPPI. So you refuse to yield to lucid reason?

ANASTASIA. I am innocent.

MISSISSIPPI. Can no logic on earth persuade you to confess to murder?

ANASTASIA. I did not kill my husband.

MISSISSIPPI (*slowly*). Then Madeleine's belief that her lover's death was due to an act of vengeance by his wronged wife, a belief which caused her such unutterable despair, was nothing but an insane fantasy?

ANASTASIA (*with shining eyes*). Your wife believed that?

MISSISSIPPI. The thought that you might have killed your husband brought Madeleine to the verge of madness.

ANASTASIA (*with barely restrained triumph*). She suffered before she died?

MISSISSIPPI. Terribly.

ANASTASIA (*jubilantly*). I achieved what I set out to do! I stabbed her to the heart! She groaned, raved, wept, cried out! She paid me back a thousandfold in despair for every second of her pleasure! I killed both of them! He perished at my hands and she through his death! They perished like beasts, they died like dogs!

(MISSISSIPPI *sits down again; so does* ANASTASIA.)

MISSISSIPPI. So you did poison your husband, Madam?

ANASTASIA. Yes, I poisoned him. We loved one another, he deceived me and then I killed him.

MISSISSIPPI. On the morning of the sixteenth of May you went to Bodo von Übelohe-Zabernsee. As a childhood friend of yours and as a friend of your husband's he gave you the poison, believing blindly that you would use it to destroy your dog, and you gave it to your husband with his after-lunch coffee instead of sugar.

ANASTASIA. He took one piece and died.

MISSISSIPPI. Did you do all that?

ANASTASIA (*with a terrible grandeur*). Yes, all of it.

MISSISSIPPI. And you do not regret your horrible deed?

ANASTASIA. I would do it again and again.

MISSISSIPPI (*white-faced*). I am gazing into an abyss of passion.

ANASTASIA (*indifferently*). Now you can take me away.

MISSISSIPPI (*rises slowly and solemnly*). I have not come to arrest you. I have come to ask you to be my wife.

(*He bows solemnly. A terrifying silence.*)

58

ANASTASIA (*her head spinning*). To ask me what?

MISSISSIPPI. To ask for your hand.

ANASTASIA. My hand?

MISSISSIPPI. I am well off, draw a very good salary, live a retiring life, am deeply religious, occupy my leisure chiefly with the collection of old engravings, for the most part idyllic landscapes which seem to me best to portray the original guiltless state of nature, and I can expect a pension fully adequate to our social standing.

ANASTASIA (*deathly pale*). That is monstrous!

MISSISSIPPI (*bows again*). Human life *is* monstrous, Madam.
   (*He sits down. As if hypnotized,* ANASTASIA *sits down too.*)

MISSISSIPPI. Could I possibly ask for another cup of coffee? (*He looks at his watch.*) I have another twelve minutes.

ANASTASIA (*mechanically fills his cup*). I find it impossible to understand your behaviour. First you force me to confess to a deed that must inevitably fill any man with horror at what a woman is capable of, and then you ask me in cold blood to be your wife.

MISSISSIPPI (*helping himself to sugar, calmly*). Let me make to you the terrible confession that I too killed my wife with the same sugar-like poison with which you killed your husband.

ANASTASIA (*after a long pause, horrified*). You too?

MISSISSIPPI (*firmly*). I too.
   (ANASTASIA *sits as though stunned.* MISSISSIPPI *stirs his coffee.*)

MISSISSIPPI. After I had confiscated the remainder of the poison from Count Übelohe – this time also there were two pieces – I went home and put one of them in Madeleine's black coffee after lunch. Half an hour later she gently fell asleep.
   (*He drinks. He puts down the cup.*)
   (*Dully*) It was the worst half-hour of my life.

ANASTASIA (*staggered*). So that is the destiny which binds us together.

MISSISSIPPI (*exhausted*). We have confessed our deed to one another.

ANASTASIA. You have killed and I have killed. We are both murderers.

MISSISSIPPI (*firmly*). No, Madam. I am not a murderer. Between your deed and mine there is an infinite difference. What *you* did in response to a dreadful impulse, I did in obedience to a moral judgment. You slaughtered your husband; I executed my wife.

ANASTASIA (*scared to death*). Executed?

MISSISSIPPI (*proudly*). Executed.

ANASTASIA. I don't know how to take your frightful words.

MISSISSIPPI. Literally. I poisoned my wife because she had earned the death sentence for her adultery.

ANASTASIA. There is not one code of laws in the world that prescribes the death sentence for adultery.

MISSISSIPPI. The Law of Moses.

ANASTASIA. That was a few thousand years ago.

MISSISSIPPI. I am firmly determined to bring it back.

ANASTASIA. You're mad.

MISSISSIPPI. I am merely a completely moral man, Madam. With the passage of time our laws have miserably degenerated. They are discounted paper money that still circulates for appearances' sake in a society whose only religion is pleasure, which has bestowed privileges upon robbery and does barter in women and oil. Only idealists out of touch with reality can still imagine that the cheque paid by Justice is covered. Compared with Old Testament law, which lays down the death penalty for *both* parties to adultery, our civil law is a wretched mockery. For this sacred reason, the murder of my wife was an absolute necessity. It was a question of reversing the course of world history, which has lost the Law and gained a freedom devoid of all moral responsibility.

ANASTASIA. Then I am completely at a loss to know why you are asking me to marry you.

MISSISSIPPI. You are beautiful. And yet you are guilty. You touch me deeply.

ANASTASIA (*uncertainly*). You love me?

MISSISSIPPI. I can no longer love.

ANASTASIA. What do you mean?

MISSISSIPPI. You are a murderess, Madam, and I am the Public Prosecutor. But it is better to be guilty than to see the guilt. Guilt can be repented; the sight of guilt is fatal. In my work I have stood for twenty-five years face to face with guilt; its look has destroyed me. I have spent whole nights begging for the power to love just *one* more person. In vain. I can no longer love what is lost, I can only kill. I have become a wild beast that springs at humanity's throat.

ANASTASIA (*shuddering*). And yet you expressed the wish to marry me.

MISSISSIPPI. It is absolute justice itself that compels me to take this step. I executed Madeleine in a private, not an official capacity. By this action I consciously offended against the existing law. For this misdemeanour I must be punished, even though my motives were as pure as spring water. But in this unworthy age, I am compelled to be my own judge. I have passed sentence. I have condemned myself to marry you.

ANASTASIA (*stands up*). Sir.

MISSISSIPPI (*likewise stands up*). Madam.

ANASTASIA. I have listened patiently to your monstrous talk. But what you have just said goes beyond the bounds of decency. You openly declare that marrying me is a punishment for the murder of your wife.

MISSISSIPPI. I wish you also to look upon marrying me as a punishment for the murder of your husband.

ANASTASIA (*coldly*). So you regard me as a common murderess?

MISSISSIPPI. You did not poison your husband out of respect for justice, but because you loved him.

ANASTASIA. Anyone else who killed her husband for love, as I did, you would have handed over to the Court?

MISSISSIPPI. I should have made it my life's ambition. In only very few cases have I failed to get a death sentence passed, and every time that happened my health suffered so severely that I was brought to the edge of the grave.

ANASTASIA (*after a long pause, resolutely*). Call the police!

MISSISSIPPI. That is impossible. By our deed we are indissolubly bound together.

ANASTASIA. I desire no mitigation of the punishment.

MISSISSIPPI. There can be no question of that. With our marriage I am not offering you mitigation, but an infinite intensification of the punishment.

ANASTASIA (*close to fainting*). You are offering me marriage in order to torture me unceasingly!

MISSISSIPPI. In order to torture *us* unceasingly. Our marriage would mean hell for both parties!

ANASTASIA. There is no sense in it!

MISSISSIPPI. You are now a murderess; through our marriage I shall change you into an angel.

ANASTASIA. You cannot compel me.

MISSISSIPPI. I demand your hand in marriage in the name of absolute morality!

ANASTASIA (*staggering behind the folding screen*). Call the police!

MISSISSIPPI. In my twenty-five years as Public Prosecutor I have obtained over two hundred death sentences, a figure that has never been remotely approached anywhere else in the bourgeois world. Is this superhuman achievement to be destroyed by a weak woman? We both belong to the highest stratum of contemporary society, Madam. I am the Public Prosecutor and your husband owned a beet-sugar factory. Let us now act like beings of the highest degree of responsibility. Marry me! Enter with me into the martyrdom of our marriage!

ANASTASIA (*yelling in a final despairing outburst*). Call the police!

MISSISSIPPI (*icy cold*). In an age when murder, adultery, robbery, incest, lies, arson, exploitation and blasphemy are not inevitably punished with death, our marriage will be a triumph of justice!

ANASTASIA (*deathly pale*). God above!

MISSISSIPPI (*monstrously*). Marry me!

ANASTASIA (*looking despairingly at the picture in the background*). François!

MISSISSIPPI. So you accept my proposal of marriage?

ANASTASIA. I accept your proposal of marriage.

MISSISSIPPI (*slips his wedding ring off his finger*). Then will you please give me the ring which you received from your dead husband.

(ANASTASIA *slips her wedding ring off her finger and places it on his finger.*)

MISSISSIPPI. Now take the ring which I received from Madeleine.

(*He puts the ring on her finger. He bows.*)

You are now my wife.

ANASTASIA (*tonelessly*). I am your wife.

MISSISSIPPI. Before the legal formalities take place you will spend six months in Switzerland. In Grindelwald or Wengen, or possibly Adelboden. Your nerves are in a bad state. The mountain air will do you good. I shall have prospectuses of the afore-mentioned places sent to you by the travel agency.

(*He rings the little silver bell. The MAID enters right.*)

My top hat, stick and coat!

(*The MAID goes out.*)

We shall be married in the Calvinist church. The legal formalities will be handled by the Minister of Justice, the ecclesiastical ones by Bishop Jensen. They are both old friends; we were undergraduates at Oxford together. We shall live here; I shall be ten minutes closer to the Court. In case there is not sufficient room for my collection of old engravings we shall build an extension. Our life will be hard. As a loyal wife you will have to stand by me in the sufferings and joys of my profession. We shall watch together the executions which I have been able to bring about. They take place on Fridays. Moreover, I shall expect you to provide spiritual comfort for those condemned to death, particularly those from the poorer sections of the population. You will take them flowers, chocolate and cigarettes, if they smoke. As far as my old engravings are concerned, attendance at a few lectures at the university should suffice. (*He bows, then with a sudden shout*) Now I shall get my death sentence passed this afternoon, that's a dead certainty!

(*He stands motionless. Silence.*)

ANASTASIA (*seizes her forehead with both hands and suddenly cries out in despair*). Bodo! Bodo!

(*She rushes out left.*)

MISSISSIPPI. This, ladies and gentlemen, took place five years ago and was the dramatic beginning of a marriage which, although it was hell – and what hell – nevertheless, and this is the important thing, had a basically ennobling effect upon both my wife and myself. I threw myself wholeheartedly into the work of the Court; Anastasia turned to stone; I exulted, justice had triumphed, and my wife grew pale as death. Unfortunately I did not hear her despairing cry of 'Bodo, Bodo' as she clutched her forehead – the incident you have just witnessed. I was already on the stairs, or possibly even in the street. A circumstance which I profoundly regret, not because I doubt my wife – I still consider her innocent and completely incapable of the heinous sin of adultery even in thought; but I should have attached more importance to the fact that she was bound by ties of pure friendship to such an excessively emotional and grossly over-imaginative Count (COUNT ÜBELOHE *staggers by outside the window*) who constituted a childhood memory to which she remained true. A great deal might then have been avoided. A great deal – not the failure of my truly monumental effort to rebuild the world from its very foundations by the application of the Law of Moses perhaps, but probably the bitter end to which we both came. Yet despite the wealth of mental suffering they imposed, the years of my second marriage were among the happiest of my life; professionally too they were blessed, for, as is well known, I succeeded in increasing the number of my death sentences from two hundred to three hundred and fifty, of which only eleven – under scandalous circumstances, being prevented by acts of clemency on the part of the Prime Minister – could not be carried out. Our marriage moved with complete regularity within the proposed orbit. As I had foreseen, my wife's character grew substantially deeper and she even acquired a more positive attitude towards religious sentiments; she watched the executions at my side with perfect calm and composure, without ever losing her natural sympathy with the victims (*a picture floats down front stage showing Anastasia watching an execution*); her daily prison visits, which soon became an emotional need for her, continually increased her desire to help, so that she was universally known as the Angel of the Prisons; in short, it was a fruitful period which brilliantly confirmed my thesis that strict laws strictly obeyed are alone capable of making man a better, nay a higher being. (*The picture floats upwards again.*) Thus a few years passed. We have shown the beginning of my marriage; let us now show the end. The room has changed little. The maid is just hanging up two engravings by Rembrandt and Seghers (*the* MAID *enters right and hangs up the engravings*); this should be enough to convey to you the atmosphere of our home. Of the rest of the engravings some are in my study through the door at the back on the right – as you see it – some in Anastasia's boudoir and bedroom, through the door on the left, and some in the hall, through the door in front on the right. Beside the crape-encircled picture of the deceased beet-sugar manufacturer, who departed this life under such unfortunate circumstances, hangs the portrait of my first wife, Madeleine, who died in a similar manner, a fair-haired, rather sentimental-looking young woman, as you can see (*the picture descends backstage next to the portrait of the beet-sugar manufacturer, which has been there from the beginning*) likewise ringed with black crape. (*The Maid has meanwhile gone out right.*) Also in the room is my friend Diego, who did not, as just now, enter through the grandfather clock – a highly improbable action; on the contrary, I brought him in through the door on the right. (DIEGO *has entered the room through the grandfather clock and is now straightening his tie in front of the mirror through which the audience can see.*) Diego occupies the position of Minister of Justice in the undefined and undefinable country in which this room is situated; Diego – this too I should like to mention – takes a profound interest in my wife's philanthropic work. He is an honorary member of the Prisoners' Aid Society presided over by my wife. You are in the picture, ladies and gentlemen, we can begin. The Minister has lit a cigar, a sign that he wants to speak to me.

THE MINISTER. It must be ...

MISSISSIPPI. One moment –
      (*He also lights a cigar.*)

THE MINISTER. It must be about five years ...

MISSISSIPPI (*again to the audience*). It is night, let us not forget that either, a gloomy November night. We are already changing the lighting, already a lighted chandelier is descending, bathing everything in a cloud of brownish gold.

THE MINISTER. It must be about five years now since you married the Angel of the Prisons.

MISSISSIPPI. The tremendous moral support I receive from my wife fills me with the keenest satisfaction.

THE MINISTER. It is indeed rare for a wife to console those whom her husband executes. Your zeal is astonishing. You have just obtained your three hundred and fiftieth death sentence.

MISSISSIPPI. One more professional triumph. Even though it was easy to bring the aunt-murderer to the gallows, no success ever did more to increase my self-confidence. You have come to congratulate me.

THE MINISTER. As a lawyer I do indeed admire you, but as Minister of Justice I am compelled to dissociate myself from you.

MISSISSIPPI. That's news to me.

THE MINISTER. Well, you see, the international situation has changed somewhat. I am a politician. I can't possibly afford to be as unpopular as you are.

MISSISSIPPI. I do not allow myself to be swayed by public opinion.

THE MINISTER. You are a genius, and judges are putty in your hands. The Government has repeatedly urged you to clemency.

MISSISSIPPI. The Government needs me.

THE MINISTER. Did need you. There is a slight difference. A high rate of death sentences was useful. It was a question of punishing political murders and restoring order. But now the best policy is to cut the ground from under the opposition's feet by modestly tempering justice with mercy again. At one moment we have to cut off heads in the name of God, at the next we must be merciful to please the devil; no state can avoid that. Once the way in which you exercised your office saved us, but now it is a danger to us. It has made us a laughing-stock throughout the Western world and has unnecessarily stirred up the extreme Left. We must take appropriate steps. A Public Prosecutor who has obtained three hundred and fifty death sentences and dares to declare in public that the Law of Moses ought to be brought back, is no longer to be tolerated. It is true that we are all rather reactionary nowadays, when you come to look at it, but in God's name there is no need to take such a radical line as you do.

MISSISSIPPI. What has the Government decided?

THE MINISTER. The Prime Minister wishes you to retire.

MISSISSIPPI. Did he depute you to convey this message to me?

THE MINISTER. That is the purpose of my visit.

MISSISSIPPI. According to law civil servants can be dismissed only when they are guilty of a felony, fraud, or associating with a foreign power or a political party that is planning the overthrow of the state.

THE MINISTER. You refuse to retire?

MISSISSIPPI. I refuse.

THE MINISTER. The Cabinet will have to compel you.

MISSISSIPPI. The Government must realize that it is fighting against the best lawyer in the world.

THE MINISTER. Your struggle is hopeless. You are the most hated man in the world.

MISSISSIPPI. Your struggle is equally hopeless. Thanks to me, you are the most hated government in the world.

THE MINISTER (*after a pause*). You know, we were undergraduates at Oxford together.

MISSISSIPPI. We were.

THE MINISTER. I can't understand how a man of your intelligence and your not insignificant origins can take such pleasure in beheading people. After all, we come of the best families in the country and that alone should make us exercise a certain restraint.

MISSISSIPPI. Exactly.

THE MINISTER. What do you mean?

MISSISSIPPI. My mother was an Italian princess and my father an American arms king, were they not? Your grandfather was a famous general who lost countless battles, and your father a colonial governor who suppressed various negro revolts. Our families caused heads to roll haphazard, I demand death for the guilty. They were called heroes, I am called a hangman. If my professional success throws an unfavourable light on the best families in the country, it only means that I am showing them up in their true light.

THE MINISTER. You are stabbing us in the back.

MISSISSIPPI. You are stabbing Justice in the back.

THE MINISTER. As Minister of Justice my job is to decide whether justice is politically feasible or not.

MISSISSIPPI. Justice cannot be changed!

THE MINISTER. Everything in the world can be changed, my dear Florestan, except man. You have to realize that before you can rule. To rule means to steer the ship of state, not to cut off heads. Ideals are all very well, but I have to stick to the possible and do without ideals except when I make a speech. The world is bad, but not hopeless; it only becomes hopeless when measured by absolute standards. Justice is not a mincing-machine but a compromise.

MISSISSIPPI. To you, Justice is primarily a slot-machine that provides you with an income.

THE MINISTER. I was best man at your wedding. But at to-morrow's Cabinet meeting I shall be forced to vote against you.

(*He puts his cigar down on the ashtray.*)

MISSISSIPPI. I have nothing more to say to the Government.

THE MINISTER. I have delivered the Prime Minister's message as deputed. Will you now please see me out?

(*They leave through the door on the right. The room is empty. Enter from the left* SAINT-CLAUDE, *now with a dark-brown goatee beard, whereas at the beginning he was clean-shaven. He is wearing rough clothes. A brown leather jacket. Is the audience mistaken in thinking that* SAINT-CLAUDE *has just come from* ANASTASIA, *whose hand he is kissing as he appears? The woman in the white nightdress may have been someone else, so fleetingly is she seen. We will leave this question open for the moment.* SAINT-CLAUDE *goes to the table, picks up the Minister's cigar, smells it, continues smoking it. Then he goes to the window backstage right and opens it. Admires the Venus. Then sits down on the left of the coffee table.* MISSISSIPPI *re-enters from the right.*)

SAINT-CLAUDE (*without looking up*). Good evening, Paul.

(MISSISSIPPI *stands motionless in the doorway.*)

MISSISSIPPI (*slowly getting a grip on himself*). You!

SAINT-CLAUDE. Yes, me. You've done it, Paul. You have become Prosecutor General, you bear the name Florestan Mississippi, you fill the newspapers with your deeds, you possess a home full of old furniture of various periods and no doubt also a beautiful wife.

(*He blows a smoke ring.*)

MISSISSIPPI. And what do you call yourself now?

SAINT-CLAUDE. Something even finer than you: Frédéric René Saint-Claude.

MISSISSIPPI. You don't seem to be doing badly either.

SAINT-CLAUDE. Yes, I've done it too. I have become a citizen of the Soviet Union, a colonel in the Red Army, an honorary citizen of Rumania, a member of the Polish parliament and a member of the Politburo of the Cominform.

MISSISSIPPI. How did you get in?

SAINT-CLAUDE. Through the window.

MISSISSIPPI. Then I'll shut it.

(*He goes backstage and shuts the window.*)

What do you want with me?

SAINT-CLAUDE. When you have been abroad for so long, the first thing you do when you get back is to visit your old friends.

MISSISSIPPI. I suppose you crossed the frontier illegally?

SAINT-CLAUDE. Naturally. After all, my job is to reorganize the Communist Party here.

MISSISSIPPI. Under what name?

SAINT-CLAUDE. The Party for People, Faith and Homeland.

MISSISSIPPI. What has that to do with me?

SAINT-CLAUDE. Well, you will have to start looking round for a new job, my dear Paul.

MISSISSIPPI (*walks slowly to the table*). What do you mean?

SAINT-CLAUDE. It seems to me you have no alternative but to comply with the Prime Minister's request.

MISSISSIPPI (*slowly sits down on the right of the table, facing* SAINT-CLAUDE). You eavesdropped on my conversation with the Minister of Justice?

SAINT-CLAUDE (*in amazement*). Good heavens, no. I simply bribed the Minister for Internal Security.

MISSISSIPPI. Such interest in me on the part of a Soviet citizen makes me feel uneasy.

SAINT-CLAUDE. You have become such an internationally

notorious figure that even we are interested in you. I have come to make you an offer.

MISSISSIPPI. I can't imagine what business we could possibly have with one another now.

SAINT-CLAUDE. The Communist Party of this country has too long been without a head. We have chosen you to fill this vacancy.

MISSISSIPPI. That is a very curious proposition.

SAINT-CLAUDE. There can be no better recommendation for the position than to have obtained three hundred and fifty death sentences.

(MISSISSIPPI *stands up and goes to the window right, where he stands with his back to the audience.*)

MISSISSIPPI. And what if I refuse?

SAINT-CLAUDE. Then we shall have to attack your weak spot.

MISSISSIPPI. I have no weak spot. No one doubts the moral seriousness of my purpose.

SAINT-CLAUDE. Nonsense. Everyone has a vulnerable spot. Yours does not lie in your attack on society, it lies in yourself. You apply to the world the measure of absolute morality, and that is only possible because the world accepts you as moral. Your effectiveness would collapse the moment the halo of your virtue was destroyed.

MISSISSIPPI. It cannot be destroyed.

SAINT-CLAUDE. Do you really believe that?

MISSISSIPPI. I have trodden the path of righteousness.

(SAINT-CLAUDE *stands up.*)

SAINT-CLAUDE (*calmly*). You forget that *I* have come back.

(MISSISSIPPI *turns round. Silence.*)

MISSISSIPPI (*deathly pale*). You're right. I never expected to see you again.

SAINT-CLAUDE. Unfortunately our meeting was unavoidable. You have not only gained yourself a pre-eminent position in society by your death sentences – you also bear the name Florestan Mississippi, claim descent from an Italian princess and have an Oxford degree. You descended upon the world like a sun, and blinded by your fire the world has never looked into your origins.

MISSISSIPPI (*panting*). Louis!

SAINT-CLAUDE. That's right, Paul! Cry out to the darkness from which you came!

MISSISSIPPI. I want nothing more to do with it!

SAINT-CLAUDE. But it wants plenty to do with you.

MISSISSIPPI. Hyena!

SAINT-CLAUDE. I'm glad to see you returning to the language that comes naturally to us. Let us not forget our noble birth. No more than five lire was paid for our begetting; the gutter ran red as we came; rats showed us what life is, their fur wet with sewage; from the vermin that crawled over our bodies we learnt how time passes, never to return.

MISSISSIPPI. Be quiet.

SAINT-CLAUDE. Come, come. Let us sit down again in your Louis Quatorze chairs.

(*He sits down.* MISSISSIPPI *comes to the table.*)

MISSISSIPPI. When we parted thirty years ago we swore never to see each other again.

SAINT-CLAUDE (*smoking*). So we did.

MISSISSIPPI. Then go.

SAINT-CLAUDE. I'm staying.

MISSISSIPPI. You mean to break your word?

SAINT-CLAUDE. Of course. Keeping one's word is a luxury forbidden to us by our origins. What are we, Paul? First we stole the rags that covered our bodies, and filthy copper coins to buy mouldy bread for our bellies; then we were forced to sell ourselves, white victims in the hands of fat bourgeois whose cries of pleasure rose to heaven like the miauling of cats; and finally – with violated backsides, but with the pride of young capitalists – we used our hard-earned money to run a brothel, I as the proprietor and you as the doorkeeper.

(*A long pause.* MISSISSIPPI *sits down.*)

MISSISSIPPI (*panting*). We had to live!

SAINT-CLAUDE. Why? If we had hung ourselves from the nearest lamp-post, no one would have raised the slightest objection.

MISSISSIPPI. Why did I put up with all that unspeakable misery if not because I found in the corner of a damp cellar a half-mouldered Bible, from which I learnt to read, night after night, frozen stiff, by the light of the gas lamps? Should I have remained alive one day longer, if the vision of the Law had not flowed over me like a sea of fire bursting into our darkness, so that henceforth everything I did, the deepest humiliation I suffered and the meanest crime I committed, served the one goal of reading law at Oxford in order to become a public prosecutor and bring back the Law of Moses, driven by the knowledge that mankind must go back three thousand years in order to go forward again?

SAINT-CLAUDE (*wildly*). Did I too not have a vision of how this world that stinks of hunger, drink and crime could be improved? This hell that resounds with the singing of the rich and the howling of the exploited? Did I not find Karl Marx's *Kapital* in the pocket of a murdered ponce? And did I not go on with the terrible life we were forced to lead merely so that one day I could bring about the world revolution? We are the last two great moralists of our age. We have both adopted a disguise. You the mask of the hangman and I the mask of the Soviet spy.

MISSISSIPPI. Take your hands off my shoulders.

SAINT-CLAUDE. I'm sorry.

MISSISSIPPI. So you too have come to blackmail me?

SAINT-CLAUDE. If you won't see sense.

MISSISSIPPI. For ten years I did a menial job in your brothel, and in return you paid for my studies. We no longer owe one another anything.

SAINT-CLAUDE. There is something that cannot be paid for: life.

You chose it and I gave it to you. I showed you the terrible crooked path that leads from beast to man, and you followed it. Now it is my turn to make demands. Not for nothing did I pick you out of the gutter. The question is whether the Communist idea is to be or not to be. You are far too promising a genius for the Party not to try and make capital out of you.

MISSISSIPPI. I fight with the same ardour against the West as against the East.

SAINT-CLAUDE. I haven't the slightest objection to that, so long as you smash first one and then the other and don't attack both at the same time. That would be utterly foolish. What matters is not our sympathies, but reality. It is our historical misfortune that of all peoples it was the Russians who adopted Communism, although they are totally unsuited for it. Now we have to overcome this disaster.

MISSISSIPPI. Naturally you don't dare to advance this theory in public!

SAINT-CLAUDE. I have the freedom of Mikoyan's house. My task is not to commit suicide, it is to carry out a world revolution. Communism is the doctrine that teaches us how man can rule the earth without oppressing men. That is how I understood it in the holy nights of my youth. But I cannot put this doctrine into effect without power. Therefore we must reckon with the powers. They are the chessmen with which we make our moves. We must know what is; we must know what we want; and we must know what is to be done. These are three difficult things. The world as a whole has become immoral. Some fear for their business, others fear for their power. The Revolution must be directed against all. The West has gambled away liberty, the East justice; in the West Christianity has become a farce, in the East Communism. Both sides have betrayed themselves; the world situation is ideal for a true revolutionary. But reason compels us to give our backing to the East. Russia must conquer so that the

West goes under, and at the moment of the Russian victory there must be a universal uprising against the Soviet state in the name of Communism.

MISSISSIPPI. You're dreaming.

SAINT-CLAUDE. I am calculating.

MISSISSIPPI. Only the Law can change the world.

SAINT-CLAUDE. You see? Now we're back in our youth again, under the wet cellar vaults. The Law! When we argued about the Law, we fought all night long, till we were both battered and bleeding, and as the grey dawn broke to find us exhausted we rolled over one another down the slag heaps. We both wanted justice. But you wanted the justice of Heaven and I wanted the justice of the earth! You want to save an imaginary soul and I a real body!

MISSISSIPPI. There is no justice without God!

SAINT-CLAUDE. There is only justice without God. Nothing can help man but man. But you staked your money on another card – on God. That is why you must now give up the world; if you believe in God man is for ever evil, since goodness rests with God alone. Why do you still hesitate? Man cannot keep God's law, he has to create his own law. We have both shed blood; you have slain three hundred and fifty criminals, I have never counted my victims. What we are doing is murder, therefore we must do it to some purpose. You have acted in the name of God, I in the name of Communism. My deed is better than yours, for I am seeking something in time, while you are seeking something in eternity. What the world needs is not redemption from sin but redemption from hunger and oppression; it has no need to pin its hopes upon Heaven, it has everything to hope for from this earth. Communism is the Law in its modern form. Why do you still perform sacrifices when I am already carrying out surgical operations? Why are you still a theologian when I am already a scientist? Throw your God into the fire and you will have humanity, the drunken dream of our youth.

MISSISSIPPI. God cannot be thrown into the fire. He is Himself the fire.

(*Silence.*)

SAINT-CLAUDE. You won't come to us?

MISSISSIPPI. No.

SAINT-CLAUDE. We need your head, as I told you.

MISSISSIPPI. That is ambiguous.

SAINT-CLAUDE. That is unambiguous. I wanted your head as an instrument, now I want it as a prize. The papers that made you a relation of the Italian royal house were forged by me. The money for your studies came from my brothel.

MISSISSIPPI. What are you going to do?

SAINT-CLAUDE. Since I cannot have you as what you could be to us, I shall take you as what you are to us – as a hangman. The masses must be whipped up. It is true that without your co-operation I think it is the silliest thing we could do; but the order has been given. There is only *one* fight that will draw the masses, the fight against the man who has obtained three hundred and fifty death sentences, among them twenty-one Communists.

MISSISSIPPI. Who were common murderers!

SANIT-CLAUDE. The Trade Unions are demanding that you should be brought to justice; if the Government refuses, they will order a general strike.

MISSISSIPPI (*slowly*). I cannot prevent you.

SAINT-CLAUDE. You cannot prevent me and I cannot change you! (*He opens the window.*) Goodbye, I shall sink down before you once again. We were two brothers who looked for each other in a night that was too dark. We shouted for one another, but we did not find each other! The chance was unique, but the moment was wrong. We brought everything with us, you intelligence, I energy, you terror, I popularity, both of us an ideal origin. What a historic pair we should have been!

(*He climbs into the window frame. The 'Internationale' is heard from outside.*)

MISSISSIPPI. Louis!

SAINT-CLAUDE. Do you hear their singing, their drunken bawling, you friend of my youth, you trembling jackal with whom I walked through the underground passages of our first years, despairing at the indifference of all men, burning for their brotherhood, do you hear the song? This is the only place where they still sing those lines with enthusiasm, the only place where they still believe them, the only place where Communism can be made into a reality and not a ghastly pretence, this is the only place. And what prevents it? God, pulled out of a heap of refuse. What a farce! Go into a lunatic asylum, Paul.

(SAINT-CLAUDE *vanishes. Silence.* ANASTASIA *enters from the left in a white nightdress.*)

ANASTASIA. Are you still up?

MISSISSIPPI. It is midnight. You should be asleep, Madame. Remember the work you have to do tomorrow in the St John's Prison for Women.

ANASTASIA (*uncertainly*). Was there somebody here?

MISSISSIPPI. I was alone.

ANASTASIA. I heard voices.

(MISSISSIPPI *goes to the window and closes it. Then he steps back into the room.*)

MISSISSIPPI. I was talking to my memories.

(*A stone flies in through the window on the left. From outside shouts: 'Murderer, mass murderer!'*)

ANASTASIA. A cobblestone!

MISSISSIPPI. Pull yourself together. There'll be more than that smashed soon!

ANASTASIA. Florestan!

MISSISSIPPI. I have only you, Madame, the Angel of the Prisons, a shield which I hold up against the whole of mankind.

(*Curtain. Light in the auditorium.* ÜBELOHE *steps in front of the curtain.*)

ÜBELOHE. Ladies and gentlemen, if I ask you not to go for the interval yet, although the lights have been switched on, if I ask you to stay for my speech, it is only because in this very intricate plot the light which I shall cast upon Anastasia's former life is as important as that which Saint-Claude's appearance has cast upon the antecedents of the Public Prosecutor. You know me, you have twice seen me floating through the air past the cypress and the apple tree. I am Count Bodo von Übelohe-Zabernsee. I have come down in the world, unquestionably. I'm drunk, as you see. I wreck the whole play, I admit that too. But I can neither be left out nor toned down. My appearance on the scene is ridiculous, out of place, like me myself, like my whole grotesque life. My sudden return is highly embarrassing, and of course there is nothing more I can do to help, as you will see. But here, at this critical point in the action into which a crafty author has drawn you, ladies and gentlemen, as an audience, and us on the stage, we must ask ourselves *how* the author became involved in all this. Did he allow himself to be carried along from one free association to another without any preconceived idea, or was he guided by some secret plan? Oh, I can well believe that he did not create me light-heartedly, under the influence of some random hour of love, that he was concerned to investigate what happens when certain ideas collide with people who really take them seriously and strive with audacity and vigour, with insane fervour and an insatiable greed for perfection, to put them into effect. Yes, I can well believe that. And I can well believe that the curious author sought an answer to the question of whether the spirit – in any shape or form – is capable of changing a world that merely exists and is not informed by any idea, that he wished to ascertain whether or not the material universe is susceptible of improvement, to investigate the truth of a suspicion which

perhaps arose in him during some sad and lonely night. This
too I can well believe. But even so, ladies and gentlemen, I
must bitterly deplore the fact that, having created us, he took
no further hand in our fate. Thus he created me, Count Bodo
von Übelohe-Zabernsee, the only one whom he loved with
all his passion, because I alone in this play take upon myself
the adventure of love, that sublime enterprise which, whether
he survives or perishes in it, endows man with his greatest
dignity. But probably for that very reason, he placed upon
me the curse of a truly ludicrous life and gave me, not a
Beatrice or a Proeza – or whatever lofty being a Catholic
bestows upon his fine, upstanding heroes – but an Anastasia,
not modelled upon heaven or hell, but only upon the world.
Thus the lover of gruesome fables and futile comedies who
created me, this stubborn Protestant with his morbid imagination, had me smashed in pieces so that he could taste my
kernel – O horrible curiosity; thus he stripped me of my
dignity in order to make me, not like a saint – saints are no
use to him – but like himself, so that he could cast me into
the crucible of his comedy not as victor but as vanquished –
the only role in which man again and again appears. And all
this merely in order to see whether in this finite Creation
God's mercy is really infinite, our only hope. But let us raise
the curtain again. (*The curtain rises. A large canvas covered with
coloured drawings screens the centre of the stage. Underneath it can
be seen the legs of* ANASTASIA *and the* MINISTER, *who are obviously embracing.* ÜBELOHE *continues in the tone of a market
salesman.*) On this canvas which has been lowered to screen
the centre of the stage we see what happened the following
day and the following night, a space of time which we shall
jump. As expected, the Public Prosecutor's position has
become grave. Top left, as seen by you, newsvendor selling
a special edition bearing the headlines: 'The Public Prosecutor
as a brothel doorkeeper.' Top right, the Prime Minister
turning pale. In the centre, Saint-Claude addressing the Trade

Unions. Bottom left, a furious mob carrying placards that read: 'Death to the three-hundred-and-fifty-fold mass murderer.' Bottom right, fellows from the police guarding the Public Prosecutor's house at night, while the sky is filled with stones being thrown at the villa; they look like flowers scattered over a red carpet. You are now in the picture. When the canvas rises you will see the room which we already know in the condition you would expect. The fin-de-siècle mirrors have been shattered. Venus has lost her head. The plaster has been knocked off the wall in places. The window-panes are in fragments. The shutters are closed; through the cracks fall the slanting rays of a sunny November morning. It is ten o'clock. I am going out into the hall on the right, where I shall press the maid to show me in. I shall wear dark glasses for the purpose. (ÜBELOHE *drops the glasses as he is about to put them on; as he bends down to pick them up he sees the legs of* ANASTASIA *and the* MINISTER. *He rises deathly pale.*) Anastasia, on the other hand, you find in a situation that embarrasses me and astonishes her. Here is the woman I love in the embrace of a man whom she must never love, at the same spot where we left her thirty-three hours ago.

(ÜBELOHE *goes out right; the canvas floats up; behind it* ANASTASIA *and the* MINISTER, *who is kissing her, become visible almost up to their heads.* MISSISSIPPI *enters from the left and pulls the canvas down again.*)

MISSISSIPPI. Before this messy canvas is finally drawn up to disclose a lying picture – the whole scene is an indecent exaggeration – my acute intelligence would long ago have divined all this, if there had been any truth in it – before this happens I should like to describe the following scene to you. (*Behind the canvas the* MINISTER *walks out backwards to the right; only his legs are seen stepping back; then the canvas rises.* ANASTASIA *is standing motionless by the table, a newspaper in her hand.*) It took place this morning. I had been working all night; this time I was trying to get a death sentence passed on a ponce – quite a tricky undertaking; outside was the raging mob, in the living-room my terrified wife. I entered the room and found the Angel of the Prisons. She was holding the special edition. The newspaper speaks the truth, I told my wife. You saw in me the natural son of an American arms king and an Italian princess. Madame, dismiss this idea from your mind, it is false, I am the son of a streetwalker whose name is as unknown to me as that of my father.

ANASTASIA. I thought for a moment, then I went up to Mississippi and solemnly knelt before him.

(*She kneels.*)

MISSISSIPPI. Deeply moved, I said: Madame, do you not despise me?

ANASTASIA. Thereupon I kissed his hand.

(*She kisses his hand.*)

MISSISSIPPI. And I said in a low voice: Madame, the purpose of our marriage has been achieved: we have done penance. Perhaps this very evening my attempts to bring back the Law of Moses will be finally shattered. You heard the tumult last night. The unworthy stones in this room, the broken mirrors, the damaged Venus speak volumes. Horrifying volumes describing a lost illusion. What is there to prevent us from publicly confessing that we are poisoners, you for love and I out of moral conviction? Then we can die a martyr's death. I am ready, Madame!

ANASTASIA. I solemnly rose and kissed his forehead.

(*She does so. The canvas descends again. Again we see the legs of the* MINISTER, *who once more approaches* ANASTASIA *from the right.*)

MISSISSIPPI. That was the scene. It staggered me and it will have staggered you. I have described it although a raging mob is now besieging me in the Court; in a few hours they will hound me through the building, up the stairs, along the galleries, down the stairs again, and finally beat me up in the entrance hall under the statue of Justice, where they will leave me streaming with blood. When this happens, I shall feel nothing but the lips of this outstanding woman – a laurel wreath flowering unwithered on my ravaged brow.

(MISSISSIPPI *leaves left.* ANASTASIA *and the* MINISTER *come into view, in a passionate embrace, as we have already seen. The room conforms to Übelohe's description. Outside, the 'Internationale'.*)

ANASTASIA. All night long they have been pelting the house with stones and singing their songs.

THE MINISTER. It was foolhardy to telephone me.

ANASTASIA. I was crazed with terror.

THE MINISTER. It is good to kiss when the world is falling apart.

ANASTASIA. You will set me free from this man. I want to go on kissing you for ever. For ever.

THE MINISTER. You shall go on kissing me for ever. One doesn't help a brothel doorkeeper.

ANASTASIA. The general strike will hit you too.

(*The* MINISTER *begins to undress. He puts his top hat on the statue of Venus, throws his coat over a chair, and so on.*)

THE MINISTER. My power is unassailable. It is not founded upon men's ardour, but upon their weariness. The longing for change is great, but the longing for order is always greater still. It will bring me to power. The mechanism is easy to see. The Prime Minister will have to go; the Foreign Minister will not be back from Washington for another hour. He will come too late. I have only to use the few minutes during which I shall be the only representative of the Government, and Parliament will proclaim me the new Prime Minister.

ANASTASIA. You will deliver my husband to the rabble?

THE MINISTER. You want him to die?

ANASTASIA. I desire his death.

THE MINISTER. You are an animal, but I love animals. You have no plan, you live only in the moment; as you have betrayed your husband, so you will betray me, and so on. For you what is will always be stronger than what was, and what will be will always triumph over the present. No one can grasp you; whoever builds upon you will perish, and only he who loves you as I love you will always possess you. No, my child! I shall not deliver your husband to the mob. I shall strike him a more radical blow than your hate could do; I shall have him put away where fools are put away.

ANASTASIA (*who has not achieved her purpose*). Please leave now. You have to go to Parliament.

THE MINISTER. It is unbearable only to meet in gaols, where prisoners and warders watch us from all sides. At least we are alone here for a change!

(ÜBELOHE *rushes in from the right.*)

ÜBELOHE (*with a voice of thunder*). Let me catch a glimpse of my beloved, Madam!

(ANASTASIA *stands thunderstruck and the bewildered* MAID *appears in the doorway.*)

THE MINISTER (*who has let go of* ANASTASIA *in dismay*). Under no circumstances must I be seen here!

(*He hurries into the room on the left.*)

ÜBELOHE (*goes to* ANASTASIA *and kisses her hand*). I beg you to forgive my reckless and unseemly entry into your private room and also my torn suit, but what is at stake is the last hope of a now utterly ruined but once noble man, the final mercy which you can show a poor soul. My name –

ANASTASIA (*cries out*). Bodo!

ÜBELOHE (*stands motionless for an instant, then he too gives vent to a blood-curdling cry*). Anastasia!

(*He staggers and sinks white-faced into the chair on the right.*)

ÜBELOHE. Some black coffee, please.

ANASTASIA (*to the* MAID). Make coffee immediately.

THE MAID (*going out right*). Heavens above, the Count!

ÜBELOHE (*deathly pale*). Forgive me, Anastasia, for not recognizing you at once, but I became exceedingly short-sighted in the tropics.

ANASTASIA. I'm sorry about that.

ÜBELOHE. It's of no importance. (*He stands up.*) You are free?

ANASTASIA. I am free.

ÜBELOHE. Pardoned?

ANASTASIA. I never went to prison.

ÜBELOHE. But five years ago I gave you poison disguised as sugar for your Pekinese, which was so fond of sweets, and you poisoned your husband with it.

ANASTASIA. I wasn't arrested.

ÜBELOHE (*staring dispiritedly into her face*). On your account I left the Continent and founded a hospital in the depths of the Borneo jungle!

ANASTASIA. Your flight was senseless.

ÜBELOHE. Was my medical licence not withdrawn?

ANASTASIA. No proceedings were taken against you.

ÜBELOHE (*tonelessly*). If the coffee doesn't come soon I shall lose my reason.

ANASTASIA (*suspiciously*). You wanted to see the Public Prosecutor?

ÜBELOHE. I came to this town from the feverish heat of the tropics on an old collier. I thought you had been condemned to life imprisonment. I intended to give myself up on condition that I could see you once more in my life. I came to this house for a permit to visit you in prison.

> (*He stares at* ANASTASIA, *who, when he looks closer, turns out to be the damaged Venus. Fortunately* ANASTASIA *has already removed the Minister's top hat.*)

ANASTASIA (*anxiously*). Bodo!

ÜBELOHE. Mississippi's address struck me as uncannily familiar the moment I heard it; so did the garden, the house, the front door, the Picasso in the hall; but my extreme short-sightedness, the hallucinations from which I have suffered ever since I had yellow fever in Batavia, left open the possibility that I was under a delusion. I know that I can no longer entirely trust my senses. I suffered from all the tropical diseases.

Cholera has dulled my memory and malaria my sense of direction. Then the maid came. It was Lucretia. I could scarcely continue to doubt, but of course much can happen in five years. Naturally she had to look for a new job. In any case, she didn't recognize me; that was probably due to my dark glasses, which I have worn since my eye infection in South Borneo. Twice I was turned away. Then I acted. I entered this room, uttered a greeting, bowed, stepped closer, kissed a hand and stood before you.

ANASTASIA. Yes, you stood before me.

(*He looks at her helplessly.*)

ÜBELOHE. Anastasia, the tropics have affected me terribly. My health is no longer good. I know that I can make mistakes, frightful mistakes. Therefore I say to myself frankly and openly, without sparing myself: Is this all the ghastly delusion of my sick brain? Or have you become the wife of the Public Prosecutor, Florestan Mississippi?

ANASTASIA (*calmly*). Yes, I am his wife.

ÜBELOHE (*cries out*). So it's true!

(*He sways.*)

ANASTASIA (*in dismay*). Bodo!

(*She clasps him; he slips down her on to the floor, unconscious. ANASTASIA madly rings the little silver bell. The MAID rushes in from the right.*)

ANASTASIA. For heaven's sake bring that coffee, my guest keeps fainting!

THE MAID. Mother of God!

(*She rushes out again. The MINISTER enters from the left.*)

THE MINISTER. I haven't a minute to lose. I must get to the government building!

ANASTASIA. My guest may recover consciousness at any moment!

THE MINISTER. There's going to be a disaster! I know there's going to be a disaster. If the Foreign Minister makes his speech before me, he will be Prime Minister.

ÜBELOHE (*slowly opens his eyes*). Forgive me, Anastasia, in my physical condition I simply can't take this continual excitement any more.

(*The* MINISTER *rushes out left again;* ANASTASIA *throws his coat and scarf after him.*)

ÜBELOHE. If I could understand just a fraction of what is going on here, I should immediately feel better. I can't make head or tail of your marriage to Mississippi.

(*He slowly rises and sits down in the chair, wiping the sweat from his face. The* MAID *enters from the right.*)

THE MAID. The coffee!

(*She puts the coffee on the table and goes out again.* ÜBELOHE *laboriously stands up. On the left, the* MINISTER *pokes his head out of the door, but darts back again when he sees* ÜBELOHE. ANASTASIA *pours out the coffee.*)

ÜBELOHE (*takes the cup, stirs his coffee, remains standing.*) A Public Prosecutor can't possibly marry a woman knowing that she has poisoned her husband.

ANASTASIA. He married me because *he* poisoned his wife.

ÜBELOHE (*stands as though turned to stone, his coffee cup in his hand*). He did?

ANASTASIA. He did. With the poison which he confiscated from you.

ÜBELOHE. In black coffee like you?

ANASTASIA. In black coffee like me. In order to bring back the Law of Moses.

ÜBELOHE. To bring back the Law of Moses.

ANASTASIA. Our marriage is supposed to be the punishment for our crime.

ÜBELOHE. The punishment for your crime.

(*He sways.*)

ANASTASIA (*vehemently*). For heaven's sake don't faint again.

ÜBELOHE. No. I'm not going to faint. At one blow the truth has turned me to stone.

(*He slowly puts the cup down on the table.*)

ANASTASIA (*anxiously*). Bodo, don't you feel well?

ÜBELOHE. Please give me some brandy.

ANASTASIA. Coffee would do you far more good.

ÜBELOHE. You can't possibly expect me to drink any more coffee in this house.

(*He sits down again.* ANASTASIA *goes silently to the sideboard and comes back with a bottle of brandy and a glass. Fills the glass. Sits down on the chair on the left.*)

I gave you the poison fully believing that you wanted to destroy your dog with it; I fled to the tropics in the deepest despair and there did penance for your crime by charitable works among head-hunters and Malays; I renounced you, whom I have loved from the beginning, in order once more to sanctify our relationship by a sacrifice; and meanwhile you marry a man whose crime is infinitely greater than mine and go on living with him in the temperate zone in the best possible social conditions and unmolested by the Law!

(*The* MINISTER *rushes across the stage from the left and out right.*)

THE MINISTER. I *must* get to Parliament, otherwise I shan't be Prime Minister!

ÜBELOHE (*amazed*). Who was that?

ANASTASIA. Only the Minister of Justice.

ÜBELOHE (*utterly bewildered*). What is a Minister of Justice doing in your house?

ANASTASIA. My life too is a hell.

ÜBELOHE. Has your whole life's work been destroyed by a woman? Have you senselessly given up a great position to flee into the miserable interior of Borneo, and have you equally senselessly returned? Have you had cholera, sunstroke, malaria, typhus, dysentery, yellow fever, sleeping sickness and chronic liver complaints?

ANASTASIA. Were you forced to watch executions every Friday? Was it your duty to go every day to visit people in prison whom your husband had condemned and who poured out the most horrible curses over you? Did you have to spend hour after hour with an unloved husband who condemned you to death without killing you? Did you have to keep the most complicated rules and the most absurd regulations, just because they were part of the Law of Moses? Do you not see that we have both suffered horribly, you physically and I mentally? You were able to flee and I had to stick it out here.

(*From the right three* CLERICS, *one Protestant, one Catholic, one Jewish, make a ceremonious entry. They bow.* ANASTASIA *rises with dignity.* ÜBELOHE, *much astonished, does the same.*)

THE FIRST. As the representative of the Synodal Council –

THE SECOND. Of the Diocese –

THE THIRD. Of the religious community of our city –

THE FIRST. We have come, honoured –

THE SECOND. beloved –

THE THIRD. gracious

THE FIRST. lady, to thank you in this grievous hour.

THE SECOND AND THE THIRD. To thank you!

THE FIRST. To thank you, for the

ALL THREE. exceptional.

THE FIRST. help, which you, honoured –

THE SECOND. beloved –

THE THIRD. gracious

THE FIRST. lady, ever bestowed upon the prisoners in our gaols. You performed this sisterly act time after time. At this critical moment may it be for you a –

THE SECOND AND THE THIRD. consolation

THE FIRST. and a source of fresh strength, a

ALL THREE. comfort in your tribulation

THE FIRST. that we not only give thanks, but also express hope.

THE SECOND AND THE THIRD. Hope!

THE FIRST. The hope that you, honoured –

THE SECOND. beloved –

THE THIRD. gracious

THE FIRST. lady, will continue to give your support to the Prisoners' Aid Society of our city. We thank you, we hope for you, we put our trust in you.

THE SECOND AND THE THIRD. We put our trust in you!

THE FIRST. To support you in your noble endeavours will now be our unceasing task.

(*They bow.* ANASTASIA *bows her head slightly.* ÜBELOHE *bows in helpless confusion.*)

THE THREE.   True, we do oppose most strongly
      Actions by your husband done.
      Unpunished must not be who wrongly
      Make the course of justice run.
      But you yourself whose succour kind
      Helped your brothers in their pain
      Please now consolation find
      In words of thanks we say again.

(*The three go out again right.* ANASTASIA *sits down.*)

ÜBELOHE (*takes his head in his hands*). That was Bishop Jensen!

ANASTASIA. They call me the Angel of the Prisons.

ÜBELOHE (*in despair, as he sinks into a chair*). And they expelled me from the Church Council!

ANASTASIA (*passionately*). Don't you see that you are the only person who can save me?

ÜBELOHE (*in surprise*). Are you in danger, then?

ANASTASIA. Now that my husband has ceased to be the Public Prosecutor he wants to give himself up to the police with me and confess our murders.

ÜBELOHE (*in dismay*). Anastasia!

ANASTASIA. This very night.

ÜBELOHE (*white-faced*). What are you going to do?

ANASTASIA (*resolutely*). I refuse to be thrust into the twilight world of the prison cells, I absolutely refuse! There is only one way to save our love, Bodo. Flee with me to Chile! It is the only country that will not extradite a murderess. After all, you're a millionaire! We'll take the plane. It leaves tonight at ten o'clock. I've made inquiries. Five years I have waited for you and now you are here. We shall be happy in Chile.

ÜBELOHE (*slowly stands up again*). We cannot flee, Anastasia. I have lost my whole fortune.

ANASTASIA (*likewise stands up, deathly pale*). Bodo!

ÜBELOHE. The tropics have completely ruined me financially as well as physically.

ANASTASIA (*with a shudder*). Übelohe-Zabernsee Castle?

ÜBELOHE. Converted into a pharmaceutical factory.

ANASTASIA. Marienzorn ob Bunzendorf?

ÜBELOHE. Auctioned.

ANASTASIA. Mont Parnasse Castle on Lake Geneva?

ÜBELOHE. Distrained upon.

ANASTASIA. Your jungle hospital in Borneo?

ÜBELOHE. Mouldered away. The native medicine proved stronger. I wanted to help mankind with love and charitable works and have become a beggar myself in the process. The torn clothes I am wearing, this ghastly jacket, this sweater knitted for me by a woman missionary in Batavia, these ragged trousers and these worn-out shoes are my only possessions.

ANASTASIA. But the St George's Hospital for the Poor belongs to you! We don't need much, Bodo. You're a doctor and I shall give piano lessons.

ÜBELOHE. Before I left, I gave the hospital to Alcoholics Anonymous.

ANASTASIA (*crushed, sinks back on to the chair*). And my husband forced me to make over all my property to the Society for Fallen Girls.

ÜBELOHE (*shuddering*). We are both ruined for good and all!
    (*He likewise sinks back on to the chair.*)

ANASTASIA. We are lost.

ÜBELOHE (*shyly*). We are not lost, Anastasia. We need only tell the truth.

ANASTASIA (*taken aback*). What do you mean?

ÜBELOHE. Have you confessed to your husband?

ANASTASIA (*mistrustfully*). Confessed?

ÜBELOHE. That you are my mistress?

ANASTASIA (*slowly*). You want to tell him that?

ÜBELOHE (*firmly*). I must tell him. I have always been extremely particular about the truth.

ANASTASIA (*resolutely*). That's impossible.

ÜBELOHE (*inexorably*). The night before François died, you gave yourself to me.

ANASTASIA. You mean that with your strict moral principles you are now going to go to my husband, five years later, and tell him that I seduced you?

ÜBELOHE. There is no other way.

ANASTASIA. That's ridiculous.

ÜBELOHE. Everything I set my hand to is ridiculous. In my youth I read books about the great Christians. I wanted to become like them. I fought against poverty, I went to the heathen, I became ten times sicker than the saints, but whatever I did and however terrible the things that happened to me, every-thing became ridiculous. Even my love for you – the only thing left to me – has become absurd. But it is our love. We must bear its absurdity.

ANASTASIA. It is always your decency that brings the most awful disasters upon us. It was the same in Lausanne. There you didn't marry me because you wanted to pass your exams first, so that a lieutenant-general was able to get me into his clutches. I seduced you; even then you refused to act. I killed François, so that at last I could become your wife; you fled to Tampang. And now you want to confess our love to the very man who poisoned his first wife as a punishment for adultery. For five years I have kept the truth from him in the clear knowledge that he would kill me if he found out. I changed myself into the Angel of the Prisons. I became a woman whom every clergyman spoke of with respect. And now you come along and want to open my husband's eyes, and at a moment that is critical enough already. It would be madness to tell him the truth.

ÜBELOHE. The truth is always madness. The truth has to be shouted, Anastasia. I shall shout it into this room, into this collapsing world of our sins. Do you want to lie, to go on and on lying? Our love can only be saved by a miracle. We must speak the truth, if we want to believe in this miracle.

ANASTASIA (*in astonishment*). You believe in a miracle?

ÜBELOHE. Our love demands a miracle.

ANASTASIA. That's nonsense!

ÜBELOHE. It is the only sense left to us. (*He lights a cigarette.*) I shall tell your husband the truth. It will burn our misery to ashes and our love will rise up, a plume of white smoke. (*He stamps out his cigarette.*) When is your husband coming back?

ANASTASIA. I don't know.

ÜBELOHE. I shall wait. Wait here among furniture and pictures. Wait till he comes.

(ANASTASIA *says nothing.*)

ÜBELOHE (*deathly pale*). Anastasia!

ANASTASIA. What is it?

ÜBELOHE. Do you love me?

ANASTASIA. I love you.

ÜBELOHE. Then come to me and kiss me.

(ANASTASIA *walks slowly towards him. She kisses him.*)

ÜBELOHE. Now I know that you will always love me. I believe in our love as I believe in the miracle that will save us.

ANASTASIA (*passionately*). Let us flee! Recklessly! Without thinking! And never return!

ÜBELOHE. No. I shall wait. I shall wait for the miracle!

PART TWO

The same room. By the coffee table, which is covered with brandy bottles, stands ÜBELOHE. *Backstage left by the window stands* ANASTASIA.

ANASTASIA. The mist is coming back.

ÜBELOHE. So is the mob.

ANASTASIA. The mist has risen from the river every evening this November.

ÜBELOHE. A Biedermeier table, two Louis Quatorze chairs, a Louis Quinze sideboard. A Louis Seize commode, an Empire sofa. I hate this furniture. I already hated it in Lausanne. I hate all furniture.

ANASTASIA (*although there has been no sound*). The cathedral is striking eight o'clock.

ÜBELOHE. Ten hours. I've been waiting ten hours.

ANASTASIA. Shots. Again and again shots.

ÜBELOHE. And this singing all the time. The kind of songs people will sing when the end of the world comes.

ANASTASIA. It will be high summer now in Chile, and at night you can see the Cross in the sky.

ÜBELOHE. Truth is the cross. I shall tell him the truth. (*He sits down at the table again.*) A Biedermeier table. Two Louis Quatorze chairs, a Louis Quinze sideboard. A Louis Seize commode. An Empire sofa. I hate this furniture. I already hated it in Lausanne. I hate all furniture.

ANASTASIA. Do you think the plane will take off in this weather?

ÜBELOHE. They fly in all weathers nowadays. Even if they smash themselves up. The truth. I shall tell him the truth.

ANASTASIA. You've drunk more than five bottles of brandy.

ÜBELOHE (*suddenly speaking wildly*). Can one put up with eleven hours of hell in any other way? Rembrandt Harmens van Rijn, 1606 to 1660, 'Landscape with Tower', etching. Hercules Seghers, 1589 to 1645, 'Old Mills', etching.

(*The two go rigid.* SAINT-CLAUDE *appears in the window on the left.*)

SAINT-CLAUDE. And while these two, man and woman, wait in their room, I, Saint-Claude, am hounding back into the gutter the friend of my youth whom I picked out of the gutter. A quiet word of command (*behind him appear men with small red flags*), and the crowd will drive the Public Prosecutor from the law courts over the bridge, round the Zwingli memorial, down towards the statue of Columbus by the docks, along the quay and into the gardens, beating and stoning him as they go – a slight movement of my hand (*he raises his hand in the air, the men disappear*), and the rabble will let him go.

(SAINT-CLAUDE *disappears. The* MINISTER *appears in the window on the right.*)

THE MINISTER. I, on the other hand, have just been elected Prime Minister. The situation appears catastrophic; foreign countries are holding their breath; U Thant is reading the newspapers with concern; Gromyko is rubbing his hands; the bottom is dropping out of the stock market; rumour is running wild; but in reality the situation is ideal for assuming power.

(*The clapping of an invisible multitude.*)

THE MINISTER. Lying on the sofa in my new office – the old Prime Minister is already in the sanatorium – I tear up the photograph of the agent smuggled in by the Cominform and throw the scraps in the fire. (*He tears up a photograph and throws the scraps in the fire.*) A fool, no more. As though a revolution directed against an individual were to be feared. You sacrifice the individual, and the bitch known as society remains untouched. That's a well tried rule – the beast called society is indestructible, if we put our money on the beast we shall stay on top for ever. (*Clapping.*) But it is important not to intervene too soon; we must profit from the apparently perilous situation created by a revolution. Think what credits America will give us if we put down a revolution that is thought to be dangerous. (*Clapping.*) The mob loves the first blood-lust, the wild hopes, the thrill of reckless destruction; but after a certain point in the revolt has been reached the masses' mood changes. If at first they were heated by the greed for more, they are now cooled by the fear of losing all. At this moment, which must be calculated exactly, one has a magnificent chance to appear as the saviour of order. (*Clapping.*) Let us profit by this. The Army is ready. Good. The police equipped with hoses. Still better. I swear by cold water. – John, a whisky. (*A servant brings a glass.*) For the time being I shall remain in the background. For the time being I shall let one fool hound another, shall let the mob rush with raised fists after our unfortunate Public Prosecutor, who at this moment is scrambling over his garden wall, filthy and spattered with blood, and now lies down under a tree – I think it's an apple tree. Too bad if they find you. Run, my dear rabbit, run. What a genius is going to perdition there.

(*He drains the glass, throws it over his shoulder and goes out. A shot rings out near by.*)

ÜBELOHE. Can you see anything?

ANASTASIA (*peers out*). There's someone lying under the apple tree.

ÜBELOHE (*rises laboriously to his feet*). Your husband?

ANASTASIA. He has got up and is limping across the terrace.

ÜBELOHE (*swaying*). I shall tell him the truth.

ANASTASIA (*steps back from the window*). Now they are shining searchlights into the garden.

(*Singing outside.*)

ÜBELOHE. And this singing all the time. The kind of songs people will sing when the end of the world comes.

ANASTASIA. He is opening the front door.

(ÜBELOHE *goes to the left of the coffee table, supports himself on it with his hands and stares spellbound at the door on the right.*)

ÜBELOHE. Do you love me?

ANASTASIA. He is about to come in.

ÜBELOHE. A miracle will take place. I shall tell him the truth and we shall be free.

(*The door on the right opens.*)

ANASTASIA (*calmly*). My husband.

(*In the doorway stands* MISSISSIPPI, *his clothes in tatters, his face smeared with blood.*)

MISSISSIPPI. Welcome to your homeland, Count.

ANASTASIA. Florestan!

(*She is about to rush to him;* MISSISSIPPI *signs to her to keep calm.*)

MISSISSIPPI. Let us not forget our guest, dear Anastasia. An attitude of unshakable calm is the only thing we can preserve in this perpetually changing world. (*He bows.*) It was five years ago last May, Count Übelohe, that I visited you in your rooms at the hospital. You will remember our conversation. It took place on a sofa under a poor copy of Raphael's 'St George'. I heard later that you had fled to the tropics. May I ask the reason for your return? You have appeared at a crucial moment for my wife and myself.

ÜBELOHE (*bowing*). Forgive me for being compelled to call upon you at such a late hour. My business is urgent.

MISSISSIPPI. You have come to give yourself up? Since my wife and I are about to take the same step, there is no longer any obstacle to your doing so.

(ÜBELOHE *pulls himself together.*)

ÜBELOHE. Mr Public Prosecutor! Five years ago you forced me, Count Bodo von Übelohe-Zabernsee, master of Marienzorn ob Bunzendorf, to leave this country. Those were difficult times for all concerned, we will not speak of them, since, Mr Public Prosecutor, I have not come to dispute with you. You married the woman to whom I gave the poison; well and good, a blow to me, a terrible blow, certainly; but you wanted to bring back the Law of Moses. I bow to such an immense passion for justice. It is a sublime thought. I bow in reverence. (*He bows.*) As an aristocrat whose forefathers fought at Pavia and Sempach, and even in the Crusades, I dissociate myself from those whose fiendish, God-forsaken singing echoes into this room. Having returned from the tropics, which bitterly disappointed me, I stand before you, Mr Public Prosecutor, ruined – I must confess – in every respect. I am not complaining. You too, Mr Public Prosecutor, as I can see, not without a shudder, by your bruised and scratched face, are ruined. It is the lot of both of us to be ruined, Sir, in this century. Ruined utterly. Decisions are no longer in our hands; history has repudiated us, you who with tireless and iron determination rose from the morass of the big city, and me, the Count, the scion of an aristocratic family. The mob is now singing your fate; mine too it will settle with mocking laughter. There is only one thing left for us to do in this foundering world – and who can still doubt that it is foundering? – one thing only and that absolute, fanatical, reckless. (*He is swaying more and more.*) We must get at the truth, Mr Public Prosecutor, to the terrible, perhaps ludicrous truth; we must stand by the truth with all our courage and all our strength.

(*He falls into the chair on the left and buries his head in his hands.* MISSISSIPPI *walks calmly to the table and rings the bell. The* MAID *enters from the left.*)

MISSISSIPPI. Bring a basin of cold water, Lucretia.

(*The* MAID *goes out.*)

ANASTASIA (*coldly*). He's drunk.

MISSISSIPPI. He will sober up and finish his speech.

ANASTASIA. Five bottles of brandy since this morning.

(*The* MAID *brings the basin.*)

MISSISSIPPI. Give the basin to the Count, Lucretia.

THE MAID. The basin, Count.

MISSISSIPPI. Dip your face in it, Count Übelohe.

(ÜBELOHE *obeys*.)

MISSISSIPPI (*to the* MAID). You can go, Lucretia.

(*The* MAID *goes out right*.)

ÜBELOHE (*slowly*). Forgive me, but it was waiting so long that reduced me to this state.

MISSISSIPPI. Go on, what is it you want to tell me?

ÜBELOHE (*stands up*). Mr Public Prosecutor! I want to tell you the truth. In my own name and in your wife's name. The truth is that your wife and I – the truth is that we – that I love your wife.

(*A tremendous burst of machine-gun fire crashes through the shutters into the room*.)

MISSISSIPPI. Back against the walls!

ÜBELOHE. The Communists.

(*A fresh burst of firing.*
All three press themselves against the walls. MISSISSIPPI *on the right,* ANASTASIA *and* ÜBELOHE *on the left. A fresh burst of firing. In the window left* SAINT-CLAUDE.)

SAINT-CLAUDE. They are already glued to the walls, pressing themselves against their sickening wallpaper. I shall smash this Louis Seize, Quinze, Quatorze furniture, the Empire chandeliers, the rococo mirrors, the engravings, vases, stuccoes, the remains of a plaster Venus, along with the sideboard it is standing on. I shall destroy all this bric-à-brac – a charcoal-burner who reduces this ridiculous world to charcoal in order to warm his coming kingdom.

(*He disappears. A fresh burst of firing*.)

MISSISSIPPI (*sharply*). Madame, go to your room. You will be safe there.

(ANASTASIA *goes out through the door on the left*.)

MISSISSIPPI (*shouting above the noise of firing*). Let us meet in the middle of the room. In view of the firing, however, I must unfortunately request you to crawl, Count.

ÜBELOHE. I'm already crawling, Mr Public Prosecutor.

(*They crawl towards the centre. A burst of firing. They duck.*)

MISSISSIPPI. Are you injured?

ÜBELOHE. Only a minor flesh wound.

(*They meet under the coffee table.*)

MISSISSIPPI. You have just made a confession, Count. As a husband, I feel obliged to put a few questions to you.

ÜBELOHE. I am at your disposal, Mr Public Prosecutor.

MISSISSIPPI. Count! Your fate is not devoid of a certain grandeur, albeit of a dubious character. Although a scion of one of our continent's oldest and most noble families, I nevertheless find you in rags. May I ask why you left Zabernsee Castle and entered what was to you an unknown world?

ÜBELOHE. I felt sorry for mankind.

(*A burst of firing. They duck.*)

MISSISSIPPI. You loved them all?

ÜBELOHE. All.

MISSISSIPPI. In their filth, in their greed?

ÜBELOHE. In all their sins.

(*A burst of firing. They duck.*)

MISSISSIPPI. Are you a Christian?

ÜBELOHE. I am a Christian.

(*A burst of firing.*)

MISSISSIPPI. What is left of your love for humanity, Count?

ÜBELOHE. Nothing but my love for your wife, Mr Public Prosecutor.

(*A burst of firing. They duck.*)

MISSISSIPPI. And what do you gain from this love for a woman who does not belong to you?

ÜBELOHE. Nothing but the hope that the soul of my beloved is not lost so long as I love her; nothing but this faith!

(*A burst of firing. They duck.*)

MISSISSIPPI. Abandon that groundless faith, Count. Love can accomplish nothing in this world. What would have become of my wife if she had only had your love? In addition to murdering her husband she would have committed adultery; I don't suppose I need say more.

ÜBELOHE. And what has Anastasia become through the Law of Moses, which you offered her?

MISSISSIPPI. An Angel of the Prisons, loved even by those whom I have condemned to death.

ÜBELOHE (*seizes hold of* MISSISSIPPI). You have no doubts about your marriage?

MISSISSIPPI. It is the most exemplary marriage of the twentieth century.

(*A burst of firing. They duck.*)

ÜBELOHE. You believe in your wife?

MISSISSIPPI. Unshakably.

ÜBELOHE. You believe that she has become better?

MISSISSIPPI. She has become better.

ÜBELOHE. You believe that there is truth between you and not fear, nameless fear?

MISSISSIPPI. I believe in her as I believe in the Law.

ÜBELOHE. You fool, whose bones I am now breaking in pieces, you clay giant into whose face I am now flinging the truth. How can you love a woman for her works? Do you not know that the works of man lie? How petty is your love, how blind your Law; *I* do not love your wife as a just woman, I love her as an unhappy one. Not as a woman who has been found, but as a woman who is lost.

MISSISSIPPI (*taken aback*). What do you mean by that?

ÜBELOHE. Sir –

MISSISSIPPI. May I ask for an explanation, Count Übelohe-Zabernsee?

ÜBELOHE. Mr Public Prosecutor, it is my duty to inform you that Anastasia was my mistress while she was still married to her first husband.

(*Deathly silence. Then orders are heard being given outside. The trampling of horses. Shrill whistles, the crowd moving back.*)

MISSISSIPPI. The revolt has been crushed. The Government has won. Rise, Count.

ÜBELOHE. Certainly.

(MISSISSIPPI *rises. So does* ÜBELOHE.)

MISSISSIPPI (*calmly*). Then my wife poisoned the beet-sugar manufacturer out of love for you?

ÜBELOHE. That was the reason for his death.

MISSISSIPPI. Open the door of my wife's boudoir, Count Übelohe-Zabernsee!

(ÜBELOHE *opens the door on the left.*)

ÜBELOHE (*uncertainly*). Are you going to ask Anastasia?

MISSISSIPPI. I consider that the most natural solution. You have accused my wife of adultery. I shall ruthlessly investigate your charge. But let us be clear about one thing: my wife's answer is going to crush one of us. Either I shall be shown up before you as a monstrous fool, or you before me as a totally degenerate alcoholic whose delirium makes his wildest wish-dreams appear true.

ÜBELOHE. I admire your objectivity.

MISSISSIPPI. Anastasia.

(ANASTASIA *appears in the door on the left and walks slowly towards the centre of the room, where she stops by the coffee table.*)

ANASTASIA. What do you want with me?

MISSISSIPPI. Count Übelohe has a question to put to you, Madame. Do you swear to speak the truth?

ANASTASIA. I swear.

MISSISSIPPI. By God?

ANASTASIA. I swear by God.

MISSISSIPPI. Now ask my wife, Count Bodo von Übelohe-Zabernsee.

ÜBELOHE. Anastasia, I have only one question to put to you.

ANASTASIA. Ask it!

ÜBELOHE. Do you love me?

ANASTASIA. No.

(ÜBELOHE *stiffens.*)

ÜBELOHE (*after a pause, reeling*). That cannot be your answer, Anastasia!

ANASTASIA. I don't love you.

ÜBELOHE. That isn't true.

ANASTASIA. I have sworn by God to speak the truth.

ÜBELOHE. But you became my mistress!

ANASTASIA. I was never your mistress.

ÜBELOHE. You gave yourself to me the night before François died!

ANASTASIA. You never touched me!

ÜBELOHE (*as though crying out for help*). But you only killed François because you wanted me to be your husband!

ANASTASIA. I killed him because I loved him.

ÜBELOHE (*slides on his knees to the table behind which* ANASTASIA *is standing*). Have mercy! Tell the truth! Have mercy!

(*He embraces the table.*)

ANASTASIA. I have told the truth.

(ÜBELOHE *breaks down.*)

ÜBELOHE (*shattered*). Beasts! You are beasts!

(*From outside, the siren of an ambulance.*)

MISSISSIPPI (*cuttingly*). You have heard the truth. Anastasia does not love you.

ÜBELOHE. Beasts! Beasts!

(*Loud knocking on the right-hand door.*)

MISSISSIPPI (*with dignity*). Count Bodo von Übelohe-Zabernsee, the insane assertions which you sucked from the breasts of the primeval forests, and which were unfortunately also inspired by alcoholic excesses, have proved devoid of all truth. Anastasia was never your mistress! By this act you have regrettably increased the number of your misdemeanours; to the unlawful supplying of a dangerous poison you have now added a gross slander, a fact which leaves no doubt that you are sinking into an ever more hopeless state not merely of physical, but also of moral degeneracy.

(*The door on the right is suddenly opened and a doctor and two male nurses enter, all in white coats.*)

THE DOCTOR. Professor Überhuber from the Municipal Hospital for Nervous Disorders.

MISSISSIPPI (*ignoring him*). Confess that you were lying.

ÜBELOHE. You are beasts!

(*Through all the doors to left and right and through the windows – from which Saint-Claude and the Minister have disappeared – and also from the grandfather clock, doctors in white coats and thick horn-rimmed spectacles throng on to the stage.*)

PROF. ÜBERHUBER. I am authorized by the Public Health Department to take you to the hospital for examination. Personal instructions from the new Prime Minister. The old one is already in our care.

MISSISSIPPI. Anastasia swore by God. Confess that you are lying, Count; I appeal to the last spark of an aristocratic sense of honour which must still be glimmering somewhere within you.

(*The male nurses seize* MISSISSIPPI.)

PROF. ÜBERHUBER. You are such an exceptionally interesting case, Mr Public Prosecutor, that I have invited the whole of the psychiatric congress here.

(*The doctors quietly clap in applause.*)

MISSISSIPPI. You were lying! Admit it! You were lying!

(*The male nurses lead* MISSISSIPPI *out.*)

MISSISSIPPI (*in despair*). Take me and my wife to the police! I poisoned my first wife and my second wife poisoned her first husband!

(*The male nurses lead* MISSISSIPPI *out.*)

PROF. ÜBERHUBER (*bows*). Don't let his words distress you, Madam. In his present remarkable state he is subject to the wildest delusions. We are quite familiar with such things. He will soon be better. Only yesterday the old Prime Minister considered himself totally incapable of governing, but today, after an electric shock and a few cold showers, he is thinking of serving his country either as an ambassador or as president of our national bank.

(*The doctors quietly clap in applause.* PROF. ÜBERHUBER *bows again to* ANASTASIA, *then goes out right. The doctors also leave through the doors and windows and the grandfather clock.* ANASTASIA *and* ÜBELOHE *are alone.* ÜBELOHE *slowly rises to his feet.*)

ANASTASIA. You told him the truth, and I betrayed you.

ÜBELOHE. Fear was greater than love.

ANASTASIA. Fear is always greater.

ÜBELOHE. And now they have come and taken your husband away.

ANASTASIA. The miracle has happened. We are free.

ÜBELOHE. And yet parted.

ANASTASIA. For ever.

ÜBELOHE. Faith is lost. A little water that trickled away into the sand.

ANASTASIA. Hope has vanished. A little cloud that turned to nothing in the light.

ÜBELOHE. Only love is left. The love of a fool, the love of a man who is ridiculous.

ANASTASIA. A love that has no further weight.

ÜBELOHE.

Henceforth I shall cry your name,
like the cry of a man with the plague
warning the wanderer, in the night into which I shall vanish.
You have cursed me, and I love you.
You have denied me, and I love you.
You have mocked the name of God, and I love you.
But from now on I shall turn away from you.
You shall never again see my face.
I am leaving you for ever.
But the love I bear you,
this love that will never grow weaker,
that has burnt me out, that has killed me,
and in whose name I am resurrected again and again,
I shall take with me.

I shall plant it in the countries through which I shall now roam,
unresting, a ruined Count, rotted by liquor,
I shall share it with every beggar.
Thus I have been flung upon a world that is now beyond
  salvation,
and nailed upon the cross of my absurdity,
I hang upon this beam
that mocks me,
exposed unprotected
to the gaze of God,
a last Christ.

  (ÜBELOHE *goes slowly out right.* ANASTASIA *stands motionless.*
  The sound of an aeroplane is heard.)

ANASTASIA. The plane for Chile has taken off.

  (*A canvas with a plane flying through clouds painted on it*
  screens the stage. SAINT-CLAUDE, *in evening dress as in Part*
  One, steps out in front of the curtain. He has a shaving towel
  round his neck.)

SAINT-CLAUDE. Let the plane fly to the highly commended
Republic of Chile. Let the Count leave too; he has given us
enough trouble. He will go under in the turmoil of the big
city, in the vast morass of liquor, perhaps through a knife in
the back, perhaps, if he is lucky, in a hospital for the poor
which he founded himself. We won't bother our heads about
him any more. Let us turn to the following morning. The
scene is sad enough. You will see for yourselves as soon as the
plane has finally vanished into the clouds. The room is in a
frightful state and ruined for good; the furniture is almost
indescribable, everything white with plaster and mortar.
You'll see. Only in the centre, unreal, obviously indestructible, stands the coffee table, still Biedermeier, laid for two
people as in the beginning; not for Anastasia and Mr Mississippi, however, but for Anastasia and me; we can't conceal
that. The fact that I now remove my beard will tell you enough.
That I am once more ruined and must start all over again,

you will have guessed. The end of the uprising was pathetic, the victory of the new Prime Minister total, the effect on my career painful. The Red Army has already reduced my rank and the Polish Parliament has withdrawn my mandate; in short, my rehabilitation is once more being cancelled and there is nothing left for me to do but to report how three people were checkmated in one game.

(*The canvas bearing the aeroplane goes up.*)
You are just hearing the first guns firing in salute from the classical temple. The city is preparing to celebrate the wedding of the new Prime Minister. (*Outside the window* DIEGO *and his* BRIDE *pass with two* CHILDREN *who are carrying the train, etc.*) You can see the exalted couple gliding past the window to the cathedral – him, whom we know well enough already, her, the new mother of the nation, the owner of the enormously popular *Evening Post*, blushing, in a wedding dress by Dior. Power has been preserved, order re-established, the old splendour and glory restored. With this festal event, with the ever renewed cheers of a happy people, the enthusiastic renderings of the combined girls' schools choir, municipal choral society and Philharmonic Association, who are bawling and blaring Beethoven's Ninth, and finally with the hollow majesty of the cathedral bells as they now start to ring, the following scene forms a painful contrast. Let us begin. (MISSISSIPPI *climbs into the room through the window on the right. He is wearing a mental-hospital uniform and disappears into his room on the right.*) That was the Public Prosecutor. He managed to escape from the lunatic asylum. Unfortunately I was not yet in the room when he climbed through the window, otherwise my friend Paul would have seen me as I shaved in front of the last fragment of this mirror, and would finally have caught on. As it was, he had no idea of my presence and I no idea of his, and by the time I had a chance to open his eyes there was no further point in it, so rapidly was he dealt with by the fate which he had prepared for him-

self. Anastasia – the equally ridiculous cause of my death – without her I should have been in safety long ago – came a little later. She had been in town, ostensibly in the St John's Prison for Women; in reality she had been trying in vain to speak to the new Prime Minister. He was not to be found – we know why. She had no alternative but to resign herself. Then she went to the bank, and now she is coming home, disguised as a charitable lady with her coat and crocodile handbag.

(ANASTASIA *enters breathless from the left.*)

ANASTASIA. Mississippi has broken out!

SAINT-CLAUDE (*indifferently*). So what?

ANASTASIA. Mental hospital nurses and police have surrounded him in the city park.

SAINT-CLAUDE. Like coursing a hare.

(*He turns round.*)

Where have you been?

ANASTASIA. In the St John's Prison for Women.

SAINT-CLAUDE. You're lying. You've been to the bank.

(*He seizes her handbag, opens it, takes out an envelope and puts it in his pocket.*)

How much?

ANASTASIA. Five hundred.

SAINT-CLAUDE. Good.

ANASTASIA. You've shaved?

SAINT-CLAUDE. Do I look different?

ANASTASIA. Yes.

SAINT-CLAUDE. Then put on your evening dress. The American ambassador is giving a party at his country house.

ANASTASIA. What do I care about the American embassy?

SAINT-CLAUDE. It's a chance to leave the city unrecognized. No one will expect me to go by that route. Why else do you think I'm wearing your husband's evening dress? (*He grips her arm and looks at her searchingly.*) I had a brilliant idea just now. We will flee together.

ANASTASIA (*anxiously*). Are the police after me?

SAINT-CLAUDE. No. They're after me. We'll go to Portugal.

ANASTASIA. Has the Party been banned?

SAINT-CLAUDE. The Party has expelled me.

ANASTASIA. What does that mean?

SAINT-CLAUDE. In response to the unerring instinct which tells it that it need fear only those who take Communism seriously, the Party will do all it can to kill me.

ANASTASIA. And what are we to do in Portugal?

SAINT-CLAUDE. Start all over again from the beginning. The world revolution that went astray in the Russian steppes must be carried out afresh from a different corner of the globe. No mean undertaking. It's a wretched state of affairs. Since the Soviet Union corrupted Communism the way it has, I have been like a man trying to blow up houses with wet dynamite. You can't send even the most miserable ruin sky-high with that.

(*He takes the little silver bell and rings it. The* MAID *enters from the right, still at her job though a bit the worse for wear.*)

SAINT-CLAUDE. Coffee!

(*The* MAID *goes out.*)

ANASTASIA (*goes up to him and gazes at him searchingly*). What are you planning to do with me?

SAINT-CLAUDE. We'll start in the sewers, rise to the doss-houses, move to the pubs and finally I shall build you a decent brothel.

ANASTASIA (*horrified*). I'm to sink to that?

SAINT-CLAUDE (*harshly*). You're to rise to that, you Public Prosecutor's wife.

(*He tears himself away and goes to the window on the left, turning his back to the audience. The* MAID *enters from the right.*)

THE MAID. The coffee.

SAINT-CLAUDE (*without turning round*). Pour out.

(*The* MAID *does so and goes out right.*)

ANASTASIA (*deathly pale, clutches at the locket hanging round her neck*). You are going to misuse me.

SAINT-CLAUDE. No. I am merely putting you to the use for which you are naturally fitted. What are you? A woman who consumes an immoderate quantity of men. In future you will live upon those against whom all revolutions have been directed – the rich. As the Angel of the Prisons you were an insult, in your new employment you will be one of the most natural means of obtaining money from the possessing class which will help to bring about its downfall. This is the only way of using you for the benefit of the world instead of its exploitation.

ANASTASIA (*opens the locket and takes out something that looks like a lump of sugar.*) You are ungrateful. I have kept you hidden in my room since the day you entered this country.

SAINT-CLAUDE. You became my mistress as an assurance against danger from our side, and I made you my mistress in order to make certain of your talents.

ANASTASIA. And if I don't come with you?

SAINT-CLAUDE (*looks at her*). Where else can you go?

ANASTASIA. The Prime Minister is my friend.

(*Cheers from outside.*)

SAINT-CLAUDE. It wouldn't do him any good to get mixed up with a poisoner just now. The only politician who can afford to have anything to do with you is I.

ANASTASIA. Are you threatening me?

SAINT-CLAUDE (*turns his back to her again*). Only for business reasons. You are the most gifted person there is for my requirements.

(*With a calm, elegant movement* ANASTASIA *stretches across the table and drops the thing like a lump of sugar into the cup on the right.*)

ANASTASIA. We shall see.

SAINT-CLAUDE. Is the coffee ready?

ANASTASIA. It's already poured out.

(SAINT-CLAUDE *comes to the table.*)

SAINT-CLAUDE. Is there any sugar in it?

ANASTASIA. No.

(SAINT-CLAUDE *takes a lump of sugar from the basin, puts it in the cup on the right, stirs it with the spoon. Puts the cup to his lips, lowers it without drinking, looks fixedly at* ANASTASIA, *puts the cup down on the table again.*)

ANASTASIA. Aren't you going to drink it?

SAINT-CLAUDE. There was sugar in it.

(*He wipes the sweat from his brow.*)

SAINT-CLAUDE. I think it would be better if I had my coffee in town, my dear. Lucky for you. It wouldn't have helped you, because the bank clerk you were going to run away with will be arrested this evening. Unfortunately he will be carrying a considerable sum of money that doesn't belong to him. As you see, I too have taken certain precautions. Go and put on your evening dress, it's time we were leaving. I'm going to fetch a car.

(ANASTASIA *goes out left.*)

So she went into her room. I gazed after her, laughed, looked at my cup with a feeling of horror, reached across the table for hers and drank it. (*He does all this.*) Oh, I knew her, the poisoned coffee remained untouched, and if my overwhelming hope of bringing about the Revolution somewhere in spite of everything had not blinded me into believing myself unrecognized as I stole a newly-stolen, freshly painted car from a garage in the dock area – the garage hands had gone off to watch the public wedding ceremony and were listening to the girls' school choir – the bagpipers were playing at the time and the Ninth was about to begin – and if, on my return through the garden I had not failed to see the three men who were rather inadequately concealed behind the apple tree and the cypress – if I had not made all these mistakes I could have become master of the whole world with the help of that invaluable woman, that whore of Babylon!

(*He leaves through the window on the right. But the room is only empty for a moment.* MISSISSIPPI *enters through the door on the*

*right. He is in the ceremonial black robe of the Public Prosecutor.
He goes to the coffee table, sees Anastasia's empty cup, fills it.
Then he slips his hand under his robe and takes out a little golden
box. Opens it. What happens now is easy to guess. He takes out
a thing like a lump of sugar, reaches across the table and drops it
into Anastasia's cup on the left. It is all done very simply and not
without elegance. ANASTASIA now enters from the left in a fiery
red evening dress. She stops dead on seeing MISSISSIPPI.)*

MISSISSIPPI *(bows)*. Madam.

ANASTASIA *(after a pause)*. Florestan!

MISSISSIPPI. You might as well call me Paul. Everyone knows
my name now.

ANASTASIA. It's madness to come here.

MISSISSIPPI. It isn't madness to want to see one's wife again before
disappearing for ever, Madame. One doesn't escape from the
madhouse twice. Won't you sit down?

(ANASTASIA *hesitates.*)

We drank coffee when we first met five years ago; now that
the time has come to say goodbye let us do the same. The
place is the same, but unfortunately sadly changed. The
wallpaper ruined, the Venus almost unrecognizable, the
Louis Quatorze, Quinze, Seize furniture smashed to pieces;
only the Biedermeier coffee table has fortunately remained
intact.

(ANASTASIA *sits down on the left*, MISSISSIPPI *on the right.*)

Would you pass me the sugar, please? *(She passes him the
sugar.)* Thank you. I urgently need a pick-me-up. My escape
called for tremendous exertions. I found the table laid for
two, Madame. Were you expecting someone for breakfast?

ANASTASIA. I was expecting you.

MISSISSIPPI. You knew I should come?

ANASTASIA. I had a premonition.

MISSISSIPPI. Then you put on that magnificent and daring dress
for me?

ANASTASIA. To receive you.

MISSISSIPPI. I don't remember seeing it on you.

ANASTASIA. I wore it the day François died.

(*She looks at the portrait.*)

MISSISSIPPI. As you see, I too have dressed in a manner worthy of our parting. I sit facing you in the robe of the Public Prosecutor. (*Watching her closely.*) Aren't you going to drink your coffee, Madame?

ANASTASIA. Yes. I'll drink it. It will do me good.

(*She drinks.*)

MISSISSIPPI (*breathes a sigh of relief*). We have now been married five years, Madam. (*He drinks.*) Good heavens, there's a lot of sugar in here.

ANASTASIA. I have done everything you demanded of me. I visited the prisoners, I comforted them and watched them die. I never forgot why I had to do it. Every day I thought of François.

(*She looks at the picture.*)

MISSISSIPPI. And I thought of Madeleine.

(*He also looks at the pictures. She watches closely as he drains his cup.*)

MISSISSIPPI. You have been faithful to me.

ANASTASIA. I have been faithful to you, as I was faithful to François.

(*She drinks up her coffee with a sigh of relief.*)

May I pour you another cup?

MISSISSIPPI. Yes, please.

(ANASTASIA *is about to pour out.*)

So you did not swear falsely, Madam?

(ANASTASIA *puts down the coffee pot.*)

ANASTASIA. Is that what you came home for? Is that why you are sitting there in front of me in that frightful cloak? Did you come to ask me *that*?

MISSISSIPPI. Yes, that is why I have come. The reasons for the death of the poor beet-sugar manufacturer are not yet clear. Madame, I shall now carry out the final interrogation.

ANASTASIA (*rises with dignity*). Sir, I am profoundly shocked that after five years of a self-sacrificing marriage you do not place more trust in me.

MISSISSIPPI (*likewise rises and bows*). Do not see in me the husband, but the Public Prosecutor who must do his terrible duty even when it involves someone he loves. Forget the hours you shared with me, your heart-warming work with the Prisoners' Aid Society. Cast out all thought of the marriage we had to lead together; physically it was hell, morally paradise. Go back in your mind to that grim afternoon on which I first visited you. Confide in me. Oh!

(*He groans, presses his hands to his right side and sinks back on to the chair.*)

ANASTASIA (*watching him closely*). Are you ill?

MISSISSIPPI. I felt a sudden violent stitch in my side, obviously of a rheumatic origin. I must have caught a chill yesterday as I lay under the apple tree. (*He stands up.*) But I feel better already. Let us continue the interrogation, Madam.

ANASTASIA. I do not understand your behaviour, Sir.

MISSISSIPPI. Do you stick to your story that you were never the Count's mistress?

ANASTASIA. I don't understand what compels you to harbour this absurd suspicion.

MISSISSIPPI. Human potentiality for evil, Madam. Count Bodo was drunk when he made his confession. In vino veritas.

ANASTASIA. I can only repeat that my childhood friend's assertion leaves me speechless and is utterly unfounded.

(*She sits down again. So does* MISSISSIPPI.)

MISSISSIPPI. You force me to take a step that I had to take once before.

(*He rings the little silver bell. The* MAID *enters from the right.*)

THE MAID. Yes, Sir?

MISSISSIPPI. Do you remember Count Bodo von Übelohe-Zabernsee, Lucretia?

THE MAID. He was a frequent visitor while the old gentleman was still alive.

MISSISSIPPI. Did Madam and the Count kiss in the manufacturer's absence, Lucretia?

THE MAID. Always.

MISSISSIPPI. You may go back to your work, Lucretia.

(*The* MAID *goes out right.*)

So you used to kiss Count Übelohe-Zabernsee in your husband's absence, Madam. Is this evidence not enough for you?

ANASTASIA. I am innocent. Call the police, if you don't believe me.

MISSISSIPPI. Since the police regard me as insane, they will not believe me. My confession that I poisoned my wife was dismissed with laughter. I have no alternative but to thrash this matter out with you on my own.

ANASTASIA. If you don't believe me, I can't help you.

MISSISSIPPI. It is impossible for one person to know another so well that he can dispense with belief, but in my case the issue is greater than that. I must be certain that you did not swear falsely. The very meaning of the Law is at stake. Our marriage was concluded in its name. The Law is meaningless if I have not succeeded in changing you, you, one single person; if throughout these five years you have been merely dissembling; if your sin, Madame, is greater than I know; if *nothing* has moved you to the depths of your soul. I *must* know what you are! An angel or a devil!

ANASTASIA (*stands up.*). That is something you cannot know; you can only believe.

(*From outside comes the beginning of the Ninth Symphony. Not as an accompaniment, but only, at infrequent intervals, a few bars for added emphasis.*)

MISSISSIPPI (*also stands up*). A sentence which in your mouth may be sacred or blasphemous, Madam.

ANASTASIA. I once more swear before God that I have spoken the truth.

MISSISSIPPI (*after a long pause, in a low voice*). Will you also swear to that if your last hour has come?

ANASTASIA (*suspiciously*). What do you mean by that?

MISSISSIPPI. If death awaits you.

(*Silence.*)

ANASTASIA (*alert*). You intend to kill me?

(*She suddenly presses her right hand to her right side and slowly sits down on a chair.*)

MISSISSIPPI. Do you not recognize the typical symptom? It generally stops almost at once, and after a while death supervenes painlessly.

ANASTASIA (*jumps up*). You have poisoned me?

MISSISSIPPI. The coffee which you drank contained the same poison with which you poisoned your husband François and I my wife Madeleine.

ANASTASIA. The coffee?

MISSISSIPPI. The coffee. Pull yourself together, Madame! We have reached the terrible conclusion of our marriage. You are facing death.

(ANASTASIA *prepares to rush out.*)

ANASTASIA. I'm going to Dr Bonsels!

MISSISSIPPI (*clasps her*). You know very well that no doctor in the world can help you.

ANASTASIA. I want to live! I want to live!

MISSISSIPPI (*embracing her with the force of a giant*). You must die!

ANASTASIA (*whimpering*). Why did you do it?

MISSISSIPPI. So that I should know the truth!

ANASTASIA. I have spoken the truth!

(MISSISSIPPI, *who has seized her by the shoulders, pushes her from right to left across the stage.*)

MISSISSIPPI. You loved only François!

ANASTASIA. Only him.

MISSISSIPPI. No other man ever possessed you? You were never an adulteress?

ANASTASIA. Never!

MISSISSIPPI. And this dress you are wearing? For whom did you dress, whom were you expecting?

ANASTASIA. You, only you.

MISSISSIPPI. You have been down to the prisoners, you have seen them lay their heads in the lap of the guillotine. Do not swear any more by God; swear by those dead to whom you now belong!

ANASTASIA. I swear!

(*In the distance is heard the final chorus from the Ninth Symphony.*)

MISSISSIPPI. Then also swear by the Law, in whose name I have been killing for thirty years, during which my hands became more and more red with blood and my soul more and more weighed down with despair and horror. Also swear by the Law!

ANASTASIA (*sobbing*). I also swear by the Law.

MISSISSIPPI. I can feel life leaving you, I can feel your body growing heavier and heavier in my arms, your face slowly turning to stone. You were beautiful and now your beauty is turning into carrion; but your soul shall not turn into carrion. Swear by your eternal bliss, swear by the immortality of your soul.

ANASTASIA. By my eternal bliss, by the immortality of my soul.

(*She sinks to the floor,* MISSISSIPPI *over her.*)

MISSISSIPPI. Then the Law is not senseless? Then it is not senseless that I have killed? Not senseless these everlasting wars and revolutions that add up to one single trumpet-blast of death? Then man does change when he is punished? Then there is sense in the Last Judgment?

ANASTASIA. I have spoken the truth.

MISSISSIPPI. How cold you are now as I embrace you; how wide your eyes are as they stare into the infinite. Is there any sense in lying now, in the sight of God? Can you be so depraved as not to speak the truth now, when you are passing over into another life?

116

ANASTASIA. I swear, I swear.

(*She lies motionless.* SAINT-CLAUDE *climbs in through the window.*)

SAINT-CLAUDE. Well, Paul?

MISSISSIPPI (*slowly*). Louis!

SAINT-CLAUDE. Have you left the lunatic asylum?

MISSISSIPPI (*slowly*). I came back for a last visit.

(SAINT-CLAUDE *goes to the coffee table and looks first at Mississippi's empty cup, then at Anastasia's empty cup.*)

SAINT-CLAUDE. Is that your wife?

MISSISSIPPI. I have killed her.

(MISSISSIPPI *stands up.*)

SAINT-CLAUDE. Why?

MISSISSIPPI. To find out the truth.

SAINT-CLAUDE. And did you find it out?

MISSISSIPPI (*comes slowly to the table, his hand pressed to his right side again*). My wife didn't lie. She wasn't an adulteress.

(*He sits down slowly on the left-hand chair.* SAINT-CLAUDE *looks at* ANASTASIA.)

SAINT-CLAUDE. Does one have to kill a woman to find that out?

MISSISSIPPI. To me she was the world. My marriage was a terrible experiment. I fought for the world and won. No one can lie when he is dying as she died.

SAINT-CLAUDE. One would have to take off one's hat to her if she could do that. It would make her a kind of saint.

MISSISSIPPI. She was the only person who stood by me, and now I also know, Louis, that I loved her.

SAINT-CLAUDE. That's no small thing.

MISSISSIPPI. But now I'm tired. I'm freezing. I feel once more the cold we felt in our youth, when I read the Bible and you Marx's *Kapital* under the gas lamps.

SAINT-CLAUDE. Those were the days, Paul!

MISSISSIPPI. Those were our best days, Louis! We were full of longing and full of wild dreams, feverish with the hope of a

better world. (*He stands up.*) I feel heavy. Lead me to my room.
(SAINT-CLAUDE *supports him.*)

MISSISSIPPI (*suddenly suspicious*). Why did you come here?

SAINT-CLAUDE. To say goodbye to you.

MISSISSIPPI. You knew I was here?

SAINT-CLAUDE. You weren't in the asylum.

MISSISSIPPI (*laughs*). Are you going away?

SAINT-CLAUDE. To Portugal. I must start all over again from the beginning.

MISSISSIPPI. We always have to start over again from the beginning. We are true revolutionaries. I shall flee with you, brother.

SAINT-CLAUDE. We belong together.

MISSISSIPPI. We'll found a brothel. I'll be the doorkeeper and you can do duty inside. Then if heaven and hell break apart, we shall plant the red flag of Justice in the midst of the tottering edifice of the world.

(*He suddenly collapses, and* SAINT-CLAUDE *lets him slide into the right-hand chair.*)

I am dizzy with fatigue. I can only see you as a shadow that is growing darker and darker. (*Collapsing over the table.*) I shan't give up. Never. All I want is to bring back the Law of Moses.

(*There is silence. Outside, the bells of the cathedral start to ring.* SAINT-CLAUDE *shakes* MISSISSIPPI, *takes away the cup, throws it on the floor, then the same with Anastasia's cup. He rings. The three* MEN *in raincoats enter from the right, their right hands in their pockets.*)

THE FIRST. You must allow us to come instead of the maid.

SAINT-CLAUDE. What do you want?

THE FIRST. You have been condemned to death, Saint-Claude. Put your hands behind your head.

(SAINT-CLAUDE *obeys.*)

Go and stand between the windows.

(SAINT-CLAUDE *obeys.*)

Turn your face to the wall. That's the simplest way to die.

(SAINT-CLAUDE *turns his face to the wall. The bells stop ringing. A shot.* SAINT-CLAUDE *stands where he is. The three* MEN *in raincoats go out right.* SAINT-CLAUDE *turns round.*)

SAINT-CLAUDE. So they fired their bullets into my body, you know the story.

(*He sits down on the right of the coffee table.*)

MISSISSIPPI (*sits upright again.*) So we perished through our own deeds, at once executioners and victims.

THE MINISTER (*appears in the right-hand window*). While I, who desire power and nothing else, embrace the world.

(ANASTASIA *has risen and goes to the* MINISTER, *who embraces her.*)

ANASTASIA. A whore, who passes unchanged through death.

SAINT-CLAUDE. But whether we too lie here in this ruin

MISSISSIPPI. Whether we die against a whitewashed wall, on a slowly sinking pyre, broken on the wheel, between heaven and earth

SAINT-CLAUDE. Again and again we return, as we have always returned

MISSISSIPPI. In ever new shapes, yearning for ever more distant paradises

SAINT-CLAUDE. Ever and again thrust out from among you

MISSISSIPPI. Nourished by your indifference

SAINT-CLAUDE. Thirsting for your brotherhood

MISSISSIPPI. We sweep by above your cities

SAINT-CLAUDE. Panting as we flap our mighty wings

MISSISSIPPI. That turn the mills which crush you.

(*In the window on the left appears* ÜBELOHE, *alone, a battered tin helmet on his head, a bent lance in his right hand, again and again submerged in the circling shadow of a windmill.*)

ÜBELOHE

Why do you raise your body from the morning mists
that lie outspread across the plain of Montiel

Why, circling your arms, do you thrust your head proudly
into the sun
which there before me
rolls up the slopes of the Catalan mountains, set free from the
   night

Look at me, windmill, giant licking your chops,
filling your belly with nations
hacked to pieces by your wing that is dripping with blood

Look at Don Quixote de la Mancha,
who knighted a drunken innkeeper,
who loves a pig-girl in Toboso

Many times battered and beaten, many times jeered at,
who yet defies you.

Forward then!

As you lift us up with your whirling hand,
horse and rider, both of them wretched,
as you hurl us into the swimming
silver of the glassy sky

I gallop on my sorry jade
away over your greatness
into the flaming abyss of the infinite

An eternal comedy

Let His glory blaze forth,
fed by our helpless futility

NOTE

Many productions, no doubt misled by the text, have made the mistake of using scenery that was too abstract. Since, among other things, this comedy is 'the story of a room', the room in which everything takes place must at the beginning be as real as possible. Only so will it be able to disintegrate. The unreal and fantastic may safely be left to the text, to the author.

DÜRRENMATT

A List of Evergreen Books

If your bookseller doesn't have these books, you may order them by writing to Order Dept., Grove Press, Inc., 80 University Place, New York, New York 10003. Please enclose cash and add 25¢ for postage and handling.